re

I THINK I CAN SEE WHERE YOU'RE GOING WRONG

Marc Burrow is a senior community moderator for the Guardian's 'Comment Is Free'. He removes comments when the CIF hits the fan. He is also a stand-up comedian in the anachronistic punk band The Men That Will Not Be Blamed For Nothing. @20thcenturymarc

I Think I Can See Where You're Going Wrong

And Other Wise and Witty Comments from *Guardian* Readers

Edited by Marc Burrows
With illustrations by Tom Gauld
With a foreword by John Crace

First published in 2014
by Guardian Books, Kings Place, 90 York Way, London, N1 9GU
and Faber & Faber Limited
Bloomsbury House, 74–77 Great Russell Street
London wc1b 3da
This paperback edition published in 2015

Typeset by seagulls.net
Printed in the UK by CPI Group (UK) Ltd, Croydon, CR0 4YY

A CIP record for this book is available from the British Library

ISBN 978-1-78335-089-6

FSC
www.fsc.org
MIX
Paper from
responsible sources
FSC® C008047

2 4 6 8 10 9 7 5 3 1

To the memory of Georgina Henry, without whose dedication and faith in the *Guardian* community this book could simply never exist.

Contents

....

Foreword

....

Below the line. Three words guaranteed to have struck fear into *Guardian* writers at some point in their careers. Before the arrival of Comment Is Free, writers had a very straightforward – dare I say, satisfactory – relationship with their readers. The writers wrote and the readers read. Occasionally a letter would arrive several days after an article appeared – usually to point out an error, though sometimes to congratulate – but for the most part there was silence. A silence into which anything could be read: a silence that writers for the most part interpreted as a sign that the article they had written was indeed the best thing to have appeared in the newspaper for some months.

Comment Is Free put an end to that particular illusion. It turned out that some readers thought the articles were completely ill-informed and the writers catatonically stupid. 'Did xxx really get paid to write this?' is a familiar below the line leitmotif. This is not a line of argument any writers really want drawn to their boss's attention. Unsurprisingly, it took time for writers to learn how to engage with commenters. Some chose, and still choose, to ignore them and make a point of never responding; others chose to get stuck in.

My own terms of engagement vary. If I am feeling a bit weedy and insecure, I try to stay away from the comments; there are some days when I don't need my all too obvious defects pointed out. If I am feeling more robust and think I have something to add, then I will join in. It has led to some curious exchanges. Shortly after I was appointed the new parliamentary sketch-writer following the death of Simon Hoggart, it was decided I should have a new byline photo as the old one was now 10 years out of date. Within days of its first appearance, at least a dozen people had commented that the new photo was horrific and frightening. 'Could I please change it?' they asked. I wrote back to say that, regrettably, I couldn't, as that was what I looked like. The only consolation I could offer was that while they could avert their eyes, I was rather stuck with it.

Some of my below the line interactions have been bruising; people are often far more blunt, rude even, online than they would dare to be face to face. But far more have turned out to be rewarding. The spikiness of the initial exchanges has turned into something more considered and nuanced; even if neither of us has admitted we were – God forbid – wrong, we have conceded the other may have a point. Several commenters have even gone on to become regular email friends. They moan to me about something, I moan back.

Mostly though, I've come to realise that below the line is a bit like being trapped in a train carriage full of *Guardian* readers and drifting in and out of hundreds of different conversations. Some are dull and predictable, some are repeats of what has been said the previous week and the week before that. But some – most frequently when commenters have long since moved off topic and started their own private/public conversation – are just riveting. As good, if not better, than anything that ever appears above the line. Intelligent, offbeat, deranged and funny. Though sometimes it's hard to work out just how intentional the humour is.

Marc Burrows has collected the finest and the weirdest below the line contributions and compiled them into the wonderful *I Think I Can See Where You're Going Wrong*. There are gems on every page. My own favourites are: 'I know someone who once drank a soy latte and six years later their car got stolen'; 'The only thing worse than checking your phone at the dinner table, save for ethnic cleansing and genocide, is pausing live football to have a smoke'; and 'Parents should not be allowed to buy books called "Baby Names". They forget that they are not naming a cute little baby; they are naming someone who they hope will become a confident happy 30-year-old. Called Sonny, or Fifi. The books should be called "Person-who-will-be-choosing-your-retirement-home Names".

You will have your own favourites. Every area of *Guardian* life is here. Seek out and enjoy.

John Crace, November 2014

Introduction

Someone forwarded me a tweet a few weeks ago. It said: '*Moderating comments on the* Guardian *website is the worst job I can possibly imagine*.' Not air traffic controller, not sweatshop worker, not even toilet cleaner in a dysentery ward on 'Madras Mondays' – they considered the worst possible job anyone could ever do, in the entire world, was having to read comments on the *Guardian* website. It's a statement that caught my attention because that is *literally* my job, and has been for the last three years. I am a senior community moderator for theguardian.com: the news and media website that by early 2014 was receiving in excess of 100 million unique visitors per month, and on a good day somewhere north of 55,000 comments. In the middle of all this is me and a small team of colleagues, trying to bring some sense of order and decency to proceedings by doing what is apparently the worst job in the entire world. Several other Twitter users agreed. It was one of those moments that cause you, however briefly, to reappraise your life choices.

You might wonder what problem anyone could possibly have with the *Guardian* comments section. Surely it's all recipes for lentil casserole and shared plans for knitting one's own yurt from leftover string and wholemeal organic noodles? Well, yes, inevitably there is a bit of that, but that's by no means the whole story. The *Guardian*'s (and indeed the *Observer*'s; for the two share the site) website has become one of the most populated platforms for online discussion in the entire world, and that inevitably means the conversational tone is set rather wide: all human life is here somewhere, ranting about the news, the weather, the football or debating the origins of Shakespeare's plays in a comment thread that runs to double the length of the Bard's complete works (a real example, by the way; only two commenters were involved). Left- or right-leaning, male or female, old or young, online communities do tend to attract commenters that passionately believe the first rule of the internet: they are completely right, and everyone else is wrong.

What's fascinating is how utterly contradictory this can sometimes make the *Guardian* community. For example, some commenters, let's call them Group A, will respond to an article about the BBC with a rant stating that the beloved corporation is a fundamentally biased leftwing nest of barely contained Marxist sedition (and *Doctor Who*). Then there's Group B, which claims that the BBC is nothing more than the mouthpiece of the Tory-led coalition, and as such a nest of rightwing reactionaries desperate to tread on the poor while propagating its agenda of iron-fisted austerity and Thatcherism (and *Doctor Who*). Obviously there's also Group C, which will chat eloquently and knowledgeably about the inner workings of the media; Group D, which will just do puns at the expense of Groups A, B and C, and Group E, which just wants to talk about *Doctor Who*.* Obviously they can't all be right, but that's not the point – the point is the conversation. The thread becomes a heaving stew of opinions, rants, jokes, facts and heartfelt declaration that Matt Smith is simply a better Doctor than David Tennant, though served badly by the scripts (this comes up even in articles about *Question Time*).

Yes it's contradictory but in those contradictions is the joy of our community. A reader is taken from the viewpoint of the initial writer, has those opinions reinforced, questioned and joked about by a group of informed and uninformed readers, is completely broadsided by a fact about something unrelated and generally has his or her day enriched, just that little bit.

Years ago this process simply didn't exist: journalism was a straightforward, one-way discourse between active writer and passive reader. The only way you could argue with an article was via the letters page (*'Dear Sir, I was startled to notice when reading your paper . . .'*) or through a bit of paper tied to a brick and heaved through the editor's window. The idea that the public could be involved in this process, that it could be a conversation as

---

* There is also Group F, whose dearest wish is to write the word 'FIRST' as the first comment under any article. This comment will inevitably appear fourth or fifth down, before being deleted by a moderator as 'Off Topic'. If I had my way, we'd also hunt down these users and ask them to take a long, hard look at the void of their lives, then pay a small fine to buy the mods a drink. Alas, this policy has yet to be approved by the *Guardian* powers.

opposed to a broadcast, seemed ridiculous, unnecessary and ultimately unthinkable, much like Lib Dems in government: a nice idea in principle, but no one expected it to actually happen.

The internet changed everything, of course. Interactivity came along; newsgroups, blogging, social media and, yes, comments at the foot of articles: the simplest and most obvious way to react to a published piece.

In the *Guardian* this began in 2006 with the launch of Comment Is Free, under the editorship of the much-missed force of nature, the late Georgina Henry. 'CIF', as it quickly became known, was named not after a lemon-scented bathroom cleaner but after a quote by the great *Guardian* editor C. P. Scott, whose most famous editorial claimed, '*Comment is free, but facts are sacred*.' Up to this point the paper's journalism had, save for the odd lively comment piece, been rooted in the second half of that statement. CIF would be different, featuring a wide range of writers who would focus on their own opinions – almost always strongly held and fiercely expressed – and allowing dissenting voices to debate the issues of the day.

What's more, *Guardian* readers would have a voice, too – almost every article would be debated 'below the line'. The articles would, at least in theory, honour the second half of Scott's famous quote, while the comments in the bottom half of the website often didn't. So successful was this arrangement, and indeed so obvious once you thought about it, that the idea spread quickly to other mainstream newspaper websites, as well as extending to the rest of the *Guardian*. Nearly a decade since the launch of Comment Is Free, which still does a roaring trade, its original format of 'article above/comments below' is ubiquitous. This has resulted not just in endless reams of comment and debate, but also in the formation of a vibrant community of *Guardian* readers sharing its thoughts and its never-ever-wrong-about-anything-ever opinions.

Strong moderation, of course, is essential. That's where the 'worst job in the world' comes in, with our department forming the thin red line that keeps the internet's Billy Goats Gruff safe from the trolls. Trolling (essentially saying something with the deliberate intention of annoying someone else) is a regular feature of online culture, and it takes many forms. The mod team exists to decide whether someone is being argumentative and opinionated or, well, being a dick. We're there to make sure people play nicely and to wipe out the insults or hate speech that inevitably appears in online discussion forums. Any internet forum, even the one on the famously partisan *Daily Mail* website, has a duty to weed out the serious trolling from its comments. We do our best to keep the deliberate derailing to a minimum and allow the genuinely interesting readers to dominate the conversation instead, as well as dealing with more spam than a Monty Python convention in a processed-meat factory.

By definition we do have to read a lot of pretty awful stuff in order to do our job and make sure the website is an interesting and fun place to visit. So why would anyone put himself through that? Why wade through other people's petty arguments and wretched opinions?

Because *Guardian* readers are *brilliant*. Honestly, they are fascinating. You can become lost in their sheer enthusiasm for the most arcane of details, their exploration of the furthest corners of erudite knowledge. They care so much about so many things, and they want you to care as well. There's the commenter who worried that installing a waterslide on Bristol High Street for a day would contribute to obesity as people wouldn't need to walk any more, or the reader who pondered whether, as a 31-year-old, he was being discriminated against because he was banned from Club 18–30 holidays. There's as much genuine wisdom below the line as there is wit, and countless articles have been enriched by added information from knowledgeable comment-ers. On the site we see forensic examinations of the facts presented in the original piece, we regularly read responses that help uncover problems on important issues such as zero hours contracts, NHS reforms and even how to deal with the nuclear leak at Fukushima. There's also some fantastically odd perspectives: a personal favourite included in this book is the commenter who made an astonishing leap of logic to argue that banning Christmas trees could prevent diabetes. What a stunning mind!

They're funny, too. Much of this book is comprised of clever people making excellent jokes – the alfresco sex enthusiast who refers to his wife as 'her outdoors', the reader who invented 'poga' (yoga on a pogo stick), or the movie fan who discredited the accuracy of a 3D-printed model of Keanu Reeves on the grounds that, in real life, 'Keanu doesn't have three dimensions.'

This is our way of celebrating this huge mass of enthusiasm, wisdom, wit and bewildering argument that has accumulated beneath our articles these past eight years and added so much to the experience of reading our work. Some of these comments have been selected because of their unintentional oddness, giving us a little glimpse into the mindset of someone, somewhere, on one particular day. Some of them have been picked because the commenter is a hilarious writer whose work deserves to be shared with as many people as possible.

The *Guardian* and *Observer* community is practically unique in internet culture. All websites, forums and blogs have trolls and ranters (the first rule, remember?), but very few have quite the glimmers of brilliance, daftness, good-natured advice and utterly sincere concerns about the biggest and smallest of issues that can be found in these pages. Please enjoy this brief snapshot of our community and remember that *Guardian* commenters are like Marmite – strongly flavoured, a little gooey but hugely enjoyable if used with moderation.

'The worst job in the world?' Not a bit of it.

Marc Burrows, November 2014

'Comment is free, but facts are sacred.'
C. P. Scott

A Note on Editing

....

Unlike comments on the website, which are never altered, some of these contributions have been edited a little to ensure they make sense on the page without the context of the original article or the rest of the conversation, and great care has been taken to preserve the meaning and intent of the original commenter. Edits have been made only where it was necessary to add a word here or there, to make the comment understandable without having to read the article above it, remove a bit of irrelevant text or to correct the odd bit of spelling or grammar. If you do spot a grammatical mistake it will be the fault of this book's editor, not the original commenter. This is the *Guardian*, after all, and we have a reputation to maintain.

1
It's Pronounced *Keen-Wah*: Food and Drink and Where to Find Them

....

Guardian readers hold many things dear – the search for peace in the troubled areas of the world, the pursuit of decent liberal values at home, and the absolute rock-solid certainty that anyone who has fish in their packed lunch at work is the spawn of Satan. A similar deep contempt is generated by people who eat Pot Noodles or can't pronounce 'quinoa' properly. Diet is an important part of any true Guardianista's thought process, and the day is not complete without a sustainably sourced soy latte.

Courses and Convenience

....

60% horsemeat? Well, that comes as a surprise to me. Based on the taste I thought they were 90% basil and oregano.

....

Who buys ready-made Bolognese?!

....

I'm sorry, but if you're going to compare small locally sourced, properly cooked food with traditions to Nando's,* you shouldn't be allowed to write about food, unless it's on the wall in McDonald's in your favourite colour crayon.

....

---

* Nando's: posh KFC.

[3]

If I get to a point where I don't think life can sink any lower, I remember any situation can be made worse by experiencing it chowing down on a Pot Noodle.

....

Sometimes I eat a Pot Noodle at my desk for lunch. The way people look at me you'd honestly think I'd sat down to eat a pot of kittens' heads. Or a small owl.

....

Findus Crispy Pancakes will always retain a special place in my heart – probably quite literally, in the form of arterial blockage.

. . . .

The Scotch egg was 1% food, 10% gristle and 89% disappointment.

Ethical Eats

. . . .

Isn't eating veal akin to having a likeness of Adolf Hitler tattooed on your face?

. . . .

Re: The effect of Western quinoa consumption on Bolivia's economy

If we can't even feel good about ourselves when we eat quinoa, we might as well eat pork eyelid burgers.

. . . .

Suppose we legally allow the poor to eat middle-class food faddists (& fascists)? This will improve their diet, adding protein from creatures that have been reared on organic lentils of the highest quality.

. . . .

All these health warnings just make the middle classes even more paranoid. I can see the day when they have to survive sucking an organic raw carrot three times a day.

. . . .

Eating meat is morally equivalent to being a non-practising paedophile who wears a prosthetic leg which, for totally frivolous reasons, is made of meat.

. . . .

It's clear that the sensible thing to do would be to ban vegetarian foods sold dishonestly as 'sausages', and require Quorn, etc., by law to be sold in different, possibly more innovative shapes.

. . . .

That's like giving up nuclear weapons in favour of biological weapons. Leave the poor goat alone. That milk wasn't meant for you.

Dining Out on Opinions

....

The chap who runs the artisan butcher in Islington told me that cheap bacon is the problem and that his imported organic pancetta is fine to eat and actually cures some minor ailments.

....

Every time I hear someone say 'quinoa' properly (*keenwah*) I think of Bridget Jones saying, 'Isn't it sad about Chech-nyaa?'

....

❶ I can't stand quinoa – it's like eating sand. Down with this sort of thing!

❷ You're supposed to cook it!

....

I'll tell you what REALLY gets up my nose: it's the weirdos that eat cauliflower. If you don't want to eat broccoli, DON'T EAT BROCCOLI. Don't go messing around with something that tastes different but is still the same shape. You lot make me sick.

. . . .

Re: Broccoli

Dreadful stuff. The black sheep of the brassica family. I'm tired of people trying to inflict it on me with their tales of its mythical health properties. I'd rather eat a boiled hedgehog.

. . . .

I was into skordalia* before it was fashionable and have nothing but contempt for hummus eaters.

. . . .

One good cauliflower cheese is worth 100 dubious beefburgers.

. . . .

---

* Skordalia: Greek foodstuff, essentially potato hummus. In Britain tends to be a posh name for a fine garlic mash.

Funny how you haven't mentioned that teff* can be seriously, and I mean seriously, flatulence-inducing. How terrible to find everyone at the dinner-party table trumpeting away through dessert . . .

Grateful Bread

....

Am I the only one who thinks that ham and cheese is a ghastly mix?

. . . .

Anyone who pays less than £2 for a loaf of bread is a total philistine.

. . . .

Poundland's toilet rolls make perfectly good organic bread substitutes.

. . . .

---

* Teff: Grain-based foodstuff originating from Ethiopia and increasingly common in UK health stores and right-on households. Like quinoa but substantially easier to pronounce.

I 'define my very being' with wholemeal bread.

. . . .

I can do an impression of a sausage sandwich with my genitalia. Certainly livened up Christmas, I can tell you.*

. . . .

As for sandwich fillings, my quotidian choice is almond butter, marmite and home-made roasted pepper and chilli.

. . . .

A wrap is not a bloody sandwich, OK? That's like trying to pass off a croissant as a pie.

. . . .

My lunch consists of black coffee and self-loathing. How do I wrap that? HOW?

. . . .

---

* Don't attempt to mimic this in public. Or in private for that matter.

I'm middle class [so] I don't bring sandwiches to work.
Thanks.

● Smoked salmon does not make one classy and rye
bread doesn't make one continental.

❷ . . . and a cake cannot be a bun . . .
though in the *Guardian* crossword it has
been and that makes me really mad.

On a personal note, anyone that puts cucumber on a
sandwich needs to be extracted from the gene pool.
Being beaten to death with a cucumber would be the
preferred and ironic method.

Why, oh why, does another person's toast smell so
much better than one's own with the same ingredients?

Resist the temptation to replace your sandwich toaster:
better the Breville you know.

A Latte Time on Our Hands

··

I know someone who once drank a soy latte and six years later their car got stolen.

···

This article doesn't mention the benefits to the smugness of people drinking Fairtrade coffee compared with those who prefer their coffee with a slight taste of blood and fear.

···

In a year's time there will be a *Guardian* article on how free camel lattes using Waitrose membership cards are putting independent artisan camel-latte retailers out of business. Or how the urge for camel milk has led to a deterioration in camel welfare.

Mashed Pun-tatos

....

❶ I watched a potato growing competition on youtuber . . .

❷ I'm gonna watch that tater . . .

❶ Spud for you . . .

❸ I have no Desiree to take part in these puns.

❹ Yeh? Well stick that in your Maris Piper and smoke it.

❺ I do miss that lovely series about King Edward.

❻ Or that other one about kings and queens and the Channel Islands – Jersey Royals?

❼ No need to have a chip on your shoulder.

❶ I'll get your jacket.

❸ You deserve a roasting for that.

❶ Mash to do about nothing.

❼ Oh Croquette! Goodbye Mr Chips.

Health and Safety

· ·

❶ There should be a special area in Hell reserved for people who use the same knife for butter and jam.

❷ Use a spoon to scoop and a knife to spread. Toast crumbs are the devil.

· ·

❶ I've had food poisoning once, so I tend to be careful. When in doubt, I'll offer a little meat to one of the cats and see what they think.

❷ We tried that. RIP Tiddles.

· ·

We have tin of haggis in the cupboard. My mother-in-law bought it for my husband when he married first time round, it's 40 years old now and a bit of a family heirloom.

· ·

I used to live on a canal boat with no fridge, just a small cupboard with a slatted door. The length of time that you can eat yoghurts after their sell-by date really shocked me.

. . . .

I found a can of confit de canard that I bought in France at the back of the pantry. The use-by date was sixteen years ago. I opened it. It was fine.

Perfect Recipes

. . . .

My recipe for the perfect egg is to let the chicken try to hatch it.

. . . .

Re: Perfect baked potatoes

❶ Simple: Stick spud in microwave, turn on high for nine minutes, eat.

❷ You are history's greatest monster.

. . . .

❶ I had one of those once. I ate the lot, had an aching stomach all evening, and then woke to a simply horrific episode of diarrhoea in the early hours of the morning which went on for quite some time.

❷ Didn't you watch *Blue Peter** when you were a kid? That was probably a hibernating hedgehog.

. . . .

My fiancé doesn't eat the skins of his baked potatoes. I'm not exactly sure what kind of depraved creature I have agreed to marry.

. . . .

Re: Perfect cheese sandwich

Unless you have access to a specialist fromager and artisan baker (and also heritage tomatoes like a marmande) then there is literally no point in trying.

. . . .

---

* *Blue Peter*: long-running BBC TV show that assumes the ideal competition prize for twenty-first century children is a small pin badge and free entry to the British Lawnmower Museum in Southport† instead of, say, an Xbox.
† A real example by the way; non-badge-holders must pay £2.

Tell me, at weekends do you dress up as a bear and chase the elderly into canals? After reading that I would believe anything.

Dos and Don'ts of BBQs

....

DO: Drink expensive imported bottled lager and ensure an all-male presence within 20ft of the BBQ.

....

DON'T: Get invited to a friend's barbeque and find yourself the only mug tending the meat, while everyone else gets pished* at the other end of the garden, finally sitting down after an hour and a half of slaving away to find all that's left is a stale roll, the runt burger you charred at the beginning and the watery bit at the bottom of the coleslaw *you* made.

....

---

* 'Pished': polite Guardianista word. See also 'bladdered', 'Inebriated', 'Dot Cottoned', 'Jeremied', 'Newcastled', 'paggered', 'plastered', 'paralytic', 'rubbered', 'spannered', 'sozzled', 'steaming', 'steampigged' or 'trollied'.

DON'T: Offer advice to the man in charge of cooking. Just eat whatever he offers and be grateful. You didn't come round for gourmet nosh; you came round to get battered in his garden.

DO: Undercook everything. It's not a barbecue unless there's very real chance of food poisoning.

❶ DO: Brown the food on the barbecue, then cook it in a microwave.

❷ DON'T: Host a BBQ. Ever. Please.

DO: Have a go at spelling 'barbecue'. DON'T: Just cop out with 'BBQ'. It's not that hard.

Our Favourite Veg-e-tables

How bizarre to go all those years without garlic butter.

When I was a child I was regularly given the raw stump from a cauliflower as a treat.

· ·

When my dad left my ma, I remember her asking why. One of his reasons, sincerely, was 'You put courgettes in everything.'

· ·

❶ I had loads of courgettes in my garden around 1981.

❷ They'll be gone off by now.

A Pizza Hut, a Pizza Hut, Kentucky Fried Chicken and a Pizza Hut, McDonald's . . .

· ·

Pret a Manger* is as grim a social phenomenon as it is a lowering gastronomic one.

· ·

---

* Pret a Manger: Posh caff.

Re: McDonald's*

Rancid industrial food thrown at you by spotty teenagers.

. . . .

Re: McDonald's vs Burger King†

Personally I wouldn't be seen dead in either. I frequent my local independent cafes and tapas bars.

. . . .

Americans should import HP Brown Sauce.‡ All of it. And keep it. Bury it if necessary.

. . . .

Krispy Kremes are flashy, urbane prettyboy doughnuts. Dunkin' Donuts are more solid, proud, working-class creations. Essentially a Ken Loach film with a Bavarian creme filling.

---

* McDonald's: Wonderful chain of eateries with very efficient lawyers. We wouldn't say a word against them.
† Burger King: Rubbish fast-food eatery. Has less efficient lawyers.
‡ HP Sauce: Tasty brown sludge, weirdly named after the Houses of Parliament, though no one as posh as a British MP would ever eat it.

2
The Joy of Sex, Health and Yoga Mats

....

Sex is a subject close to the hearts (and somewhere slightly further south, biologically speaking) of many of our readers. However, if there's one thing they like more than sex it's yoga, cycling and telling people how to have sex. Every week the *Guardian* runs at least three columns that essentially boil down to sex advice, the most notable of which is *Sexual Healing*, the weekly agony-aunt column written by noted sexpert and one-time comedian Pamela Stephenson. Every week her good advice is torn to shreds by well meaning commenters who are only too happy to discuss what goes where, in whom and how to avoid friction burns from your yoga mat.

Don't Worry, Be Happy

....

Re: The January blues

Depressed? Many people are just relieved, if not elated, to have the whole ordeal of Christmas and New Year behind them.

....

Re: How to beat the Monday blues

A tad pretentious, but we have office poetry every Monday as a tool to combat the despond.

....

❶ If a placebo can make people feel better and improve quality of life, why can't homeopathy?

❷ Placebo had one decent song. End of.*

---

* Placebo: glam-indie-rock band formed in the mid 90s whose gender-bending singer, Brian, is responsible for a whole generation of male music fans having to think long and hard about their 'preferences'. They did indeed have one good song.

I recommend six to eight glasses of homeopathy a day. It'll do wonders for your complexion.

Yoga*

....

I'm just about to launch 'poga': it's like yoga, but on a pogo stick.

. . . .

Re: Voga – a craze combining yoga and vogueing

A complete insult to the art and culture of vogueing.

. . . .

My partner and I have multiple joint problems that we attribute to over-enthusiastic yoga practice when younger.

. . . .

I find knitting much more relaxing than yoga. Mostly because knitting rarely ends up with me attempting a headstand.

---

* Not a character in *Star Wars*.

I usually have a yoga mat slung over my back and ride a vintage Gerber bike that I bought when I was working in Zurich. I guess I stand out because of the yoga mat, I've met only one other person with a mat.

. . . .

The yogic community I am involved with has succeeded in combining knitting and yoga. A knitting circle has been established where anyone can knit a garment for a small child. These are taken to an economically challenged community in India where the children receive beautifully made jumpers, beanies and scarves. Last year we shipped two suitcases of lovingly knitted wearables for kids, some of whom sleep with the goats to keep warm. The programme continues and I intend to try to knit a jumper soon. Doing so would probably help with my meditation practice as well as observing the thoughts as I learn a new skill.

The Joy of Sex (Solo)

Re: Masturbation

❶ Could we have a large print version of this article, please?

    ❷ I'm an artisanal masturbator. All done by hand, and no out-sourcing.

❸ Masturbation weakens your muscles, causes anaemia, and depletes your selenium, zinc and copper, which causes iron deficiency. This in turn can lead to bad eyesight, and even blindness.

The Joy of Sex (in Company)

The fluffy, corrupted Westernised version of tantra involves pleasant tasks like pleasuring oneself in front of a mirror or stroking one's partner with a feather. In the East it involves contemplating rotting corpses and excrement. I am running a series of weekend workshops in exploring the latter. Corpses provided, but please bring your own lunch.

At 72 years of age I have cut down on the amount of sex I have by 50%! The very small-wattage halogen bulbs in our bedside lamps have not had to be changed for over three years so we are not causing much environmental damage with our mutual pleasuring. We don't want to do our thing in the glare of two – or even one – 40-watt bulbs either.

I recall my grandmother saying with great concern that she hoped I would never have sex before marriage. 'Of course not,' I told her. I had no intention of ever getting married.

. . . .

❶ All this talk about shagging has just reminded me how frustrated and miserable I am for the lack of shagging in my life (not through lack of trying) . . . I think I'm going to have to drown my sorrows in half a bottle of Jack Daniels now.

        ❷ I think I can see where you're going wrong.

. . . .

❶ You might be wondering where condoms fit in.

        ❷ You are doing it wrong: they fit on.

. . . .

Sex is a divine union with the beloved, nothing could be better than that . . . To find your Shekinah and join her in a blissful union.

. . . .

Re: Is anything better than sex?

❶ (Quoting *Conan the Barbarian*) Crushing your enemies, seeing them driven before you, hearing the lamentation of their women.

❷ That IS how I have sex.

. . . .

The only time I told someone there was anything better than sex, it was having seen Britain's first, and so far only, golden-winged warbler (a tiny jewel of an American bird) near Tesco's car park at Maidstone, on 14 February 1989. The adrenalin rush was phenomenal.

. . . .

Re: My neighbour can hear me having sex

❶ Turn on the radio quite loudly and just ignore them!

❷ We used to live TWO floors up from a guy who used to entertain a string of handsome young men at his place. To mask (rather poorly, I might add) the sounds of them getting to know each other better, he would play *Ride of the Valkyries* loudly for the duration. On a record player. Which sometimes skipped.

❸ An old flatmate of mine used Pachelbel's *Canon*.

❹ I bet that blew the neighbours away.

Slimmers' Corner
(So Long and Thanks for All the Crisps)

....

Re: Okinawa diet could help you live to 100

❶ I would rather choke on a slice of cake tonight than live out the rest of my days eating tofu. Nothing is worth tofu.

❷ I am in Japan, and may I suggest you look up 'tofu hamburg' as a starting point? It may just help to change your mind.

❸ My uncle lived to 115 and all he ever ate was smug vegans. He said they tasted stringy and bitter.

❹ I am currently suffering my third Tory-led government; it already feels like I have lived 100 years.

....

Re: The worst diets

❶ I'm on two diets. Tried one and found it wasn't enough food.

❷ I'm on the whisky diet. I've lost two weeks already.

....

10% of our body mass isn't human, but bacterial, and those bacteria are mainly essential to life. If detoxing really worked you'd be dead.

Eating earth is called geophagy (from Greek), and has been around for a very long time. Probably healthier than the processed crap filling the aisles of our supermarkets.

An onion a day keeps everybody away.

Yoghurt, berries and nuts are my saviours.

. . . .

I've been taking a homeopathic ebola vaccine for years and I haven't had it once. Not ONCE. You're all just scared because you don't understand it.

. . . .

Ran 48 miles yesterday, off road and with some brutal hills, an absolutely perfect Sunday! Gentle bike ride and swim today (yoga is off due to public holiday).

. . . .

I have a whole beetroot first thing in the morning in a smoothie with avocado, walnuts, coconut oil, banana, ginger, kale and carrot. Doesn't taste great tbh, but I feel magnificent afterwards! Beetroot's good for men's sexual health too apparently, because of the vasodilatory, nitric oxide effect.

Posh PE, Spoons and Sack Races

....

My niece hates normal PE but does stay fit doing the school Zumba class.

....

Re: Parents' races at sports day

I've never seen anything as grossly competitive as when a famous celebrity father turned up at our school to be faced with a conspiracy of other parents – all of whom had taken drink. One of the mothers created a diversion by flashing him at the 25m mark while a couple of his fellow competitors 'accidentally' drifted into his lane, stumbled in a dribbling mess and brought him down. The plan worked like a dream – one trophy never to appear in the cabinet at home in the mansion.

....

The only time I ever won a race was when I found out that the winner got an ice-cream. It was my school sports day 1971 and it was the potato and spoon race – I had no strategy except that I walked and everyone else ran and dropped their spuds. I won the race because everyone else were looking for their potatoes all over the track. I picked a choc ice. It was all downhill from then on.

....

These things are character building and have made me what I am today: a quivering unconfident wreck.

The Gym

....

The only thing I lift is pints of cider as my five portions of fruit a day.

....

I decided to lose weight and go to the gym on realising that when you are 55 years old, buff and svelte-like, there is a great deal of pleasure to be had in being a smug bastard.

....

Suzanne Moore is getting into shape, Nick Cohen has a new haircut and is getting trim . . . Am I right in thinking there's a *Guardian* columnist vs *Guardian* columnist cage fight in the offing?

....

I tried a new machine at the gym for about 45 minutes, but I had to stop as I felt really sick. I'll probably use it again though, it's excellent. It has Mars Bars, crisps, chocolate and everything.

Gym Jams and Work Out Radio?

....

Survivor – 'Eye of the Tiger'. I haven't worked out since 1982.

....

The first movement of Beethoven's 'Eroica' often accompanies my jog around the park – inspirational, energetic and quite beautiful. That way, if I decide to expire at some point in the run, I have the wonderful second movement, *Marcia funebre* – the funeral march – to gently pulse through my ears as I take my last.

....

My gym helpfully plays the same annoying music over and over again. My motivation on the treadmill is that I'm running after the person that chooses the music.

....

The only 'soundtrack' I need on my morning perambulations is NATURE'S OWN DAWN CHORUS. The music of the English countryside – the stout yeoman on his way to God-honest toil 'neath the sun's rays, the babbling brook's merry procession, and the strident cock's dawn salutation.

Fifty Shades of Fun

....

Re: Teaching teenagers about kinky sex

Let's teach them maths, reading and financial management first.

....

Thanks for explaining 'BDSM'* – I assumed it meant something like 'Business Development and Sales Manager'. I clearly spend far too much time at the office and too little time with the wife.

....

---

* BDSM: Actually stands for Bondage, Discipline and Sadomasochism. You might prefer the commenter's version though. Why not try both?

Obviously Max Mosley should become the *Guardian*'s agony aunt: 'Like smacks? Ask Max!'*

. . . .

Funny how 'lights off' is ultimate vanilla, but invest in a blindfold and suddenly you're Captain Kinky.†

. . . .

Whenever I see the word 'peccadillo' I always think of a small, Amazonian ant-eater. In a gimp suit.

. . . .

❶ When I was at university a housemate got me a set of different-sized butt plugs‡ as a 'joke'. I have them stored in an old pillowcase because I'm too scared to throw them away in case anyone sees them. How do you dispose of butt plugs?

❷ Use them as doorstops?

. . . .

---

* Er . . . you'll have to look this up yourselves.

† Not, alas, a character in the next Avengers film.

‡ Butt plugs . . . er, you can look this up yourself as well. Probably best not to do it at work.

❶ America would be a much happier place if people carried vibrators instead of guns.

And bank robberies would be hilarious.

> ❷ Try hunting boar with a vibrator.
> You may end up with a new porcine friend,
> but it won't put bacon on the table.

. . . .

So now we have the phrase 'butt Plug' openly displayed in the title of an article on a major news outlet. We are all witnessing the decline and fall of Western thought and culture.

3
The Only Way Is Ethics: Modern Living and Moral Quandaries

....

For the Guardianista life is never simple. Yes, we have organic hummus for lunch, but is it the right sort of organic hummus? What is its carbon footprint? Could we not have bought British? Can you even get British hummus? Is asking for British hummus offensive to Middle-Eastern people? What does choosing non-indigenous hummus say about my child's development? Is he racist because he won't eat it? Should I buy the Fairtrade Kit Kat for his pudding, even though I disapprove of Nestlé's policies on baby milk in Africa, or should I buy the Mars Bar which isn't Nestlé but also not Fairtrade? Does that make me a bad parent? Can anyone recommend a book on good parenting? Is it on recycled paper? These questions go on and on and on, because life is an unending ethical minefield in which no one ever really manages to do the right thing all the time, which is why most people are desperately in need of a stiff gin and tonic and a nice sit-down.

First-World Problems

....

Re: Ad campaign about problems in the developing world

I hate it when meaningful ad campaigns make me feel like a selfish privileged elite.

....

I have been successfully growing various herbs in my kitchen window for many years, but for some reason or other I have always failed to grow rocket. The seeds germinate, but after reaching about 5 cm simply die.

....

My least favourite queuing experience was for the gondola in Bulgaria. It was a daily 45–60-minute, ill-tempered scrum, and when you got up the mountain the skiing was pretty shit.

....

Why has my download speed dropped from 75 Mbps to 63 Mbps?

I have terrible luck converting pasta sauces into gnocchi sauces.

. . . .

❶ I did have a plant next to my router and its leaves turned brown and dropped. Coincidence?

> ❷ My router is placed near some house plants
> and has stopped working.

. . . .

I just can't seem to source any freshly prepared harissa for my cous-cous.

. . . .

Since they stopped stocking classical music I can never find enough books, CDs or DVDs I like in W. H. Smith to make use of their 'Three for £17' deal.

. . . .

The sushi situation in Dublin is very dire.

Dilemmas

....

Re: Travelling back in time to kill Hitler

Wouldn't a more *Guardian* idea be to go back even further in time and be nice to him as a child?

....

Genuine question: How does a Catholic vegan square eating the flesh of Jesus with their dietary requirements?

....

❶ I have just about the most politically incorrect hobby it is possible to have. I collect antique and historic weapons and lecture on the subject.

❷ Ha, you lose. I have a complete collection of Robertson's Golly badges,* although I don't lecture on them (or, it has to be said, wear them in public).†

❶ Actually, I've got a couple somewhere from my childhood. At least you don't get called a 'baby killer' for owning a jam badge.

---

* Inexplicably racist logo featuring a 'golliwog' doll on olden-days jars of marmalades and jams. The past was a strange place.
† We're relatively sure the commenter isn't suggesting he wears them in private either. But you never know.

Of course it is – Tony Blair manages it very well.

. . . .

The worst lie a parent can tell their child: any fact said with absolute certainty.

. . . .

What's to respect in someone who tries to sit in a reserved seat?

Eco-Living

. . . .

There's plenty of other planets out there for us to ruin after this one. The technology to take us there will be ready in around 40 years. I'm trying to use up as many of the earth's resources as possible before then.

. . . .

Cotton bags can last a lifetime and be passed on to your children and possibly even your grandchildren.

. . . .

We have just decided to change our 40th-anniversary present from an exotic trip to a new but much needed, locally made kitchen.

. . . .

You can't recycle a polar bear.*†

* My polar-bear skin rug suggests otherwise.
† It's actually panda.

Humans should improve the quality of their faecal matter by forgoing all drugs, especially hormones, antibiotics and chemotherapy and eat organic foods only, so their stools will make better fertiliser.[*]

. . . .

As long as you have a house, mains power and a vehicle you cannot be living ethically; 'slightly less destructively' is the best you can hope for unless you start living in a tent and foraging.

Eco-Dying

. . . .

I have donated my body to teacher-training universities. Cremation is only adding to global warming.

. . . .

Hopefully the Port of Southampton will approve my planned Viking funeral. The ship will be made from recycled wood of course.

. . . .

---

[*] This commenter doesn't half talk some crap.

Wouldn't it be great if our dead bodies were all burned to help heat hospitals or pensioners in their homes?

....

If we were to compost humans instead of normal burial or cremation, it would help mitigate the drains on fossil sources of fuel and fertilisers.

Shopping

....

Where can you get decent vegan sandals?

....

I say remove Easter eggs and all unnecessary consumer items in a time of ecological crisis.

....

Re: Valentine's Day ethics – how green is your red rose?

I'm sure the wife will be as pleased as punch with a pair of locally sourced, fully vaccinated goats.

....

What I want to know is: what's the carbon cost of the development and distribution of this 'ethical' app, taking into account the manufacture and distribution of the iPhone?

. . . .

I'm unemployed right now but even I can still swing the extra few bob for organic, Fairtrade tea.

. . . .

Go to a fine chocolate shop and buy gourmet eggs in a paper box. Fill out the sweetness quota with dried mangoes, pears and apricots. Add a little carrot halwa. Candy some rose petals or violets. Hard-boil eggs and dye them with cabbage. Whatever you make at home, don't let it be a failed imitation of sickly sweet plasticky stuff. Make it solid, real, genuine. Enjoy the celebration of spring's arrival.

. . . .

Some of us still get milk in reusable glass milk bottles from a milkman – so no waste there.

. . . .

What about ethical shop*lifting*, how's that doing? Just because I'm too skint to afford food doesn't mean I don't have ethics you know.

. . . .

Re: Ethical eggs

❶ I'm chickening out of this debate.

❷ Eggsactly.

❸ I've had just about an oeuf of these puns . . .

❷ But I was only yolking!

❹ Let's lay this one to bed right now please.

❺ No, I want them to capon coming.

❻ A capon pun? You cock.

❹ A cock? He needs to find a chick then he'll have no need to pullet.

Equality

....

I close my eyes when I come to page 3 while reading
the *Sun* . . . am I helping the cause?

. . . .

How would any child understand 'sexism' in toys, unless
they also understood Freud's work on gender?

. . . .

Re: Gender-specific colours

Instead of worrying about pink and blue we could start
by getting rid of the misandrist* and sexist lyrics found
in nursery rhymes.

Animal Rights

....

If cod really is headed for extinction, I'd be bloody
stupid not to eat it while I still can.

. . . .

* Misandry: sexism against men. If we're honest, not really all that
common.

It is racist to compare reds and greys? Also, any person who advocates trapping and eating squirrels should be dragged behind a bus.

. . . .

Feeding 5000 people with two fish and five loaves isn't really that impressive. Whale sharks can weigh over 20 tonnes, and so getting thousands of decent-sized portions out of them is straightforward. The loaves presumably went into some kind of breadcrumb batter.

. . . .

The European eel has been hunted to extinction by the Cockney. Never mind global warming – who will look after the humble eel and its magical life journey, so our children's children may marvel at its magical magnetic feat? Fyi I can put an eel into a trance. Shame of it is, I can't find one.

. . . .

I sometimes wonder: why will people struggle to preserve orang-utans, but will not struggle to get democracy?

. . . .

Re: Ethical animal feed

As a hobbyist pig finisher,* I used to go around the neighbours seeking out 'waste' fruit and veg. Problem was you couldn't guarantee there was no meat involved, which made it difficult.

. . . .

Re: Morrissey's† campaign to stop seal-killing in Canada

People behaving like predators is quite normal and easy to understand. People being a Morrissey fan: now there is something truly beyond comprehension or justification.

I'm Dreaming of a Right Christmas

. . . .

Re: What happens to your Christmas tree once Christmas is over?

Mine becomes a log pile behind the trampoline and mulch underneath it.

. . . .

---

* Arguably the single best opening gambit to a sentence in the history of the written word.
† Morrissey- former singer with The Smiths, sporter of quiffs, quips and a bit of an old misery.

Quoting from the article, 'But real trees still appear
to be a greener choice than artificial ones' – glances
over at artificial tree, *panics* – 'which would need to
be kept for 10 years to be lower carbon.' Glances over
at 10+-year artificial tree that's still holding its own,
relaxes again. Nothing like the roller-coaster ride of
being a *Guardian* reader, eh?

....

Christmas trees are a stupid 'tradition' and a waste
of resources. We'd do better to use the land to grow
proper woodlands so we could give biodiversity a
chance, while producing a sustainable fuel, construction
materials, etc., and have more places for recreation so
people could get exercise and fresh air, and reduce
their risk of developing heart disease or diabetes.

Gardening and the Good Life

....

❶ Where can we get white eggs nowadays?

❷ Dulux.

....

❶ To save money I set a lettuce on fire till it becomes chard.

❷ I can't afford cabbage at the moment. I'm absolutely brassica.

❸ But does it salsify your appetite?

❹ With jokes leek this, you are really boiling us.

❺ Where are these jokes sprouting from?

❻ Can we all just stop digging?

. . . .

Re: Chelsea Flower Show

I'd give the prize to the garden which had a proper washing line, a swing, and space for kids to run around in. Too many designer gardens look like centrepieces for cemeteries.

Modern Etiquette

One day when I was on the London underground the lady next to me started making friendly conversation. This was so unusual and surprising I almost fell off my seat.

Re: Self-checkouts

❶ The human cashiers shift your shopping faster than the robots, and presumably they are getting paid.

❷ Unexpected Luddite in the bagging area.

Re: Shopping

❶ The best tills for speed and efficiency are Aldi's tills. They have a person who knows the price of everything.

❷ They may know the price of everything, but I bet they know the value of nothing.

They are a godsend for buying tampons though. The computer doesn't look disgusted with you as often.

· ·

The only thing worse than checking your phone at the dinner table, save for ethnic cleansing and genocide, is pausing live football to have a smoke.

· ·

If someone is being rude to you – just imagine them naked. It won't stop them but in many cases it will lighten your mood.

The Big Questions

· ·

Re: Should I buy prescription drugs over the internet?

No. The Internet is for recreational drugs.

· ·

Re: Is it OK to fake an orgasm?

Yes, yes, yes, yes!!

· ·

Re: How to deal with 'chuggers'

I reply with the Estonian phrase for 'I'm sorry, I don't speak English but how much is this pair of trousers?' It has always worked so far.

. . . .

Re: Are hot tubs an unethical waste of energy?

As a saxophonist who writes meditation music, I find a hot tub contributes a lot to my general feeling of relaxation, helps me make more effective decisions and also helps me to compose relaxing music.

. . . .

Re: Are loom bands an environmental problem?

My three-year-old has been trying to make ethical loom bands out of pasta hoops. Can't say with any real success. We're going to try the more upmarket calamari option next.

. . . .

Re: After a pay cut we had to sack our cleaner. Now nothing is being cleaned! What do we do?

Christ! Don't sack the cook or you'll both starve.

. . . .

Re: Is my house making me ill?

❶ Yes! Microwave radiation is constantly emitted in our dwellings and those of our neighbours by computer routers, mobiles, baby monitors, cordless phones, and of course microwaves.

❷ I have combated all the above by encasing myself, family, friends and my house entirely in tin foil.

· ·

Re: Is there a use for horse chestnuts aside from conkers?

They teach children about accepting life's little let-downs. The polished treasure they found under the tree on the way home from school and put in their bedroom soon turns into a dull wooden bead they have no use for. Ah well.

· ·

Re: Why are orange-ish slugs now more common than black slugs?

Have you not seen *Orange is the New Black*?

· ·

Re: Why does beer taste better from a straight glass?

Never mind that, last year CAMRA held a beer festival in a venue that only served beer in plastics. Insanity.

. . . .

Re: Do we really need to warm the teapot?

❶ No. In fact, you can dispense with the teapot entirely and just make it straight in the mug.

❷ I suppose you *could*. But why would you want to?

. . . .

Re: Why do my neighbour's leaves always land on my drive?

Your neighbours are evil wizards, and hate you.

. . . .

Re: Where do all the missing single socks go?

Socks are the larval form of wire coat hangers – no one buys wire coat hangers, yet they multiply in your wardrobe.

4
Drones and Droning On:
Technology and Its Uses

....

New moderators are always surprised by how partisan the Tech section can be. The most obsessive football supporter or the most committed religious zealot has got nothing on your average Apple or Google fan, who thinks his or her particular shiny white bit of bleepy plastic is a substantial improvement on their neighbour's shiny white bit of bleepy plastic, despite them being fundamentally identical in their shiny white bleepy plasticity, and if you don't believe them they'll bloody well tell you why. They rarely come to physical blows, but they have been known to 3D-print* some nastily graphic dioramas.

---

* 3-D printing: using a machine to create real-life, replicated models out of chemical substances. Possibly witchcraft.

Video Games

I have been known to play Battlefield 4 wearing a tweed flat cap. It does little to improve my performance, but it does make me look rather dashing, like a gentleman soldier.

I punched a cow in Grand Theft Auto V to see what happened. Games are getting so realistic now I actually felt bad about it when it mooed and rolled over. I've never done it since. Poor little cow.

Re: Airlines relaxing rules about tech use

Not too comforting to know that the pilot is busy playing Angry Birds.

Pacman has seen MILLIONS of ghosts devoured for nothing more than some glacé cherries. It's the crime that everyone knows and NO ONE is doing a thing about!

....

Insisting that 'art games' aren't games is pretty much like saying *Koyaanisqatsi* isn't a film because it doesn't have explosions in it.

....

Lone gaming is for people who aren't good enough for Counterstrike.

....

I think it's a little sad to play football on the Wii when there is open space outside on which to play football.

#socialmedia

....

Re: UKIP member suspended over sending racist tweets while drunk

❶ Never go on Twitter when you are drunk.

❷ Or racist.

❶ I'm shortly going to be launching an Anti-Social Media app which will, across any platform, tell everybody else to eff off and mind their own business.

❷ I think that's just Twitter, isn't it?

· ·

Despite having fewer than 10 followers, my father thinks his Twitter account is some sort of international message board. He uses it to advertise second-hand cars. It's not a lucrative business.

· ·

Re: Do your parents embarrass you on Facebook?

❶ It's actually a weight off when they join Facebook and stop emailing you video attachments.

❷ I have not yet embarrassed my teenage daughter but I reserve the right to do so, with the many 'cute' childhood photos I have of her, if she doesn't tidy her room.

❸ My children embarrass *me* on Facebook with their spelling.

❹ I *correct* my kids' spelling on Facebook.

No one I respect has a Facebook page.

. . . .

I'd like to state the incomprehension and fury I feel at seeing hashtags on Facebook. Why?!

. . . .

Twitter is just a condensed version of everything awful in popular culture.

Inspect-a-Gadget

. . . .

Re: Using Google Glass*

Will all the glancing upwards give me a wrinkly forehead?

. . . .

---

* Google's latest invention is 'Google Glass' – the company is so intent on making our lives more efficient they've shortened the word 'glasses' to give us more time in the day. Google Glass is a smartphone built into a pair of spectacles, and make you feel (a) terrifyingly like you're living in the future and (b) a bit of a prat.

❶ Wow! What a milestone in the technological revolution – glasses that will tell you how to make peanut-butter cookies.

❷ You got a problem with cookies?

❸ I have, but I've set my browser to block them.

. . . .

Selecting the best wearable tech is like trying to pick the best communicable STD.

. . . .

I'm only getting one when I can use it to speak with my car to discuss how to catch criminals.*

. . . .

I would not pay out three hundred quid for a watch with a plastic strap.

---

* Readers of a certain age will recognise this reference to the hit TV show *Knight Rider*, in which David Hasselhoff talked to his car through his watch, and no one thought he was mad.

Re: Apps and gadgets keeping you up to date with news, etc.

It feels a bit like we are connected to everything except other people.

· ·

Re: Rapper Dr Dre's* 'Beats' headphones

As a middle-class man who owns many cardigans, I can't really get away with wearing the same headphones as Dr Dre.

· ·

❶ I don't have a phone and I never use the internet.

❷ So how did you read the *Guardian* online and post this comment?

❸ Don't tell him, Pike!†

· ·

Re: The price of smartphones

❶ A cheaper Apple, please?

❷ You can get them for about 40p in Lidl.

---

* Dr Dre: rapper. Not a real doctor.
† A reference to a classic episode of the vintage British sitcom *Dad's Army*. For reference the scene in question is easy to find on youtube and absolutely worth your time.

I've invented a machine that'll wash all that annoying soap off your computer before it does any damage. I'm calling it the 'What Idiot Thought This Was a Great Idea?' cloth.

． ．

I presume the ultimate goal is to have an iWatch on each wrist, Google Glasses on your head with an iPad strapped to your chest, screen outwards. You can then say 'I am a ro-bot' in a silly voice.

． ．

Re: Siri and voice-activated phones

Before it was possible it seemed amazing. Now it's possible it's banal and unremarkable, used for trivial functions of consumption.

． ．

Why pay for headphones when you can play bass-driven music through the speakers on your mobile phone? Preferably on public transport with your feet on seats, with badly fitting clothes from Foot Locker.

---

* This is a real thing.

One would hope that a 'teachers' leader' would have actually said, 'Take iPads *from* children at bedtime.' If not, it certainly explains the poor standards of English seen by universities and businesses.

. . . .

I got my mum an iPad Mini when she'd broken her foot and couldn't get upstairs to the office. I don't think she's used anything else since! Mind you, her computer needs are essentially 'check email' and 'order Waitrose'.

. . . .

I swear by my pineapple corer, which makes a fiddly job easy and leaves you with a classy receptacle for your pina colada.

. . . .

I have a Squire & Sons (Made in England) tin opener that I bought in Dallas, Texas, in 1974 and have used since. I wish to be cremated with it, and a can of tuna in oil.

. . . .

Re: 'Smart' fridges

I dread the day my fridge gets smart. It will probably report me to social services.

. . . .

Re: Square egg maker

❶ Is there a device that makes round eggs?

❷ It's called a chicken.

. . . .

Quarry tiles make excellent impromptu pizza stones in an emergency.

. . . .

Re: Should I upgrade my record player?*

This guy already has the most essential h-fi component – a wife who tolerates a vinyl collection.

. . . .

Nothing shouts '*Come Dine with Me* contestant' louder than a home ice-cream machine.

---

* Record player: an MP3 you can make an ashtray out of.

❶ I for one welcome a CCTV system developed by a company whose business model is selling your personal data.

❷ Does it have a lens that glows a sinister shade of red?

. . . .

In trying to decipher a setting on my washing machine in Russian, Google translated it as 'squeeze the plums'. Beyond the call of duty for a washing machine, I'd have thought?

. . . .

Our latest toaster has a defrost button and it is a boon. The gluten-free bread I make myself curls badly if toasted straight from frozen.

How To Be Annoying on the Net

. . . .

Sending emoticons to your mum is fine because she's impressed the internet can do a smiley face. Sending one to a client, regardless of the informal nature of the email, is a crime.

. . . .

People sending emails with read receipts should have their computers forcibly removed. If I want to ignore an email that I've opened, I will.

. . . .

Our physical world is emptying. 99% of the population is connected by a curious thread of compulsion to screens, which they cannot and will not break. Nobody knocks on a door, nobody shouts in the street, save when they are drunk; even then they are doomed to be photographed and have their embarrassing image made screen-ready. We are deeply alone, in the midst of permanent and instant connectedness. Do not expect answers, for we are never at home, or at ease.

. . . .

It took me ages to figure out why people think that various things are less than three: '<3'.

. . . .

❶ Is 'lol' still allowed?

❷ Of course not, lmao.

. . . .

❶ Scrolling down my contact list I once chose 'Snowden, Edward' and not 'Snowden, Eric' when sending round a few documents about this and that. It was OK though, I don't think anyone noticed my error.

❷ I didn't think I had made any embarrassing email gaffes. But just contacted GCHQ and they told me I had made lots of them . . .

❸ I once sent a naked picture to everyone in my address book. Not only was it embarrassing, it also cost a fortune in stamps.

❹ Sending a group email to the Really Very Important people at work, I signed it off with 'Regards' as I normally do. Have you ever noticed that the 'g' key and the 't' key are quite close together on a keyboard? Can you think about what happens if your finger slips ever so slightly when typing that one, simple word? That was quite a moment.

❺ Someone I knew once sent a letter, 'Yours faithfukky' . . .

❻ After a number of high-profile incidents of the 'reply to all' nature, the very large law firm I used to work for introduced a system where if you want to send an email to an external participant on any email-reply chain it would trigger series of prompts: Are you sure you want to send this to an external participant? Y/N

Are you really really really sure? Y/N
We are so sacking you if you mess this up! Y/N

. . . .

Emoticons are the communications equivalent of
fluffy dice.

. . . .

My response to emoticons being a substitute for real
communication: :(

. . . .

I Skyped* my GP and said I thought I had a virus. He
said to have a scan, and if that didn't work, try taking it
into PC World.

. . . .

Thanks to Skype I've shared details with complete
strangers on other sides of the planet. Namely the
American Security Services.

. . . .

---

* Skype: video chat, like on *Star Trek* but with added yells of 'I
can't see you, is your camera on? Can you see me? Can you call
me instead?'

The Robot Uprising Draws Closer

Re: Household appliances gaining sentience and taking over the world

We certainly need clarification of what the legal position is if a human is slain by white goods. Maybe no case to answer, if the guarantee has run out?

Re: Internet-connected appliances gaining sentience

Trust me, this is totally escapable if you live in rural Wales . . .

❶ I popped a wholemeal slice into my Russell Hobbs toaster and the voice of Linda Snell from *The Archers* emerged, lecturing me on the importance of having regular vaginal swabs. Like most people I had mine removed when I left the council house and moved into a semi-detached.

❷ Removed what? Your vagina, or your toaster?

❶ Well they both have a 'pop-up' function. God, isn't technology marvellous?

. . . .

❶ Listen. Understand. That Terminator is out there. It can't be reasoned with; it can't be bargained with. It doesn't feel pity or remorse or fear and it absolutely will not stop. Ever. Until you are dead.

❷ Sounds like my mum.

. . . .

I worry that if all this technology starts communicating with itself, it will already be one step above me on the evolutionary ladder as I still have not been able to communicate with girls, and I'm told they are the same species as me.

. . . .

❶ A smart-fridge, that refuses to open after being emailed by your smart-clothes to say that the wearer is getting a bit porky, would be annoying.

❷ 'Open the Pad Thai door, HAL!' 'I'm sorry, I can't do that right now, Dave . . . I can't let you endanger the mission . . . to keep your trousers fitting properly. I'm shutting down Pasta Support now. Goodbye, Dave.'

Essentials for Modern Living

....

I could often murder my alarm clock. Justifiable homicide?

. . . .

Re: Dishwashers

In a few centuries time they'll look back at us and ask, 'How could they be so lazy as to waste precious energy on an expensive machine just to wash dishes?' Plus they are lousy for poaching salmon, despite some claims to the contrary.

. . . .

We are sorry. Your eCar cannot currently be started. Windows is searching for a new driver.

....

Re: Batteries made from sugar

Would it work with aspartame?

....

Corn tastes best when soybean miso is spread on it. So, I wonder, would corn be a better biofuel if miso was added to it?

....

Instead of inventing washing machines that can be switched on via a mobile phone, allowing you that precious extra hour at work, couldn't these sadists come up with some labour-saving devices that allow us a little more time with those we love?

3D Printing

....

I would like to be the first to welcome our new 3D-printed overlords.

....

❶ This printed Keanu Reeves doll actually has more facial expression than the real one.

> ❷ I didn't know Keanu Reeves HAD three dimensions?

....

Re: 3D-printed food

I thought fast food was already being printed and that's why it tastes like cardboard soaked in mayonnaise.

The Robot Overlords Get Closer

....

Re: What happens when machines become sentient?

Well, judging by the current state of my computer they'll probably just stop working.

....

Re: Drones

❶ Drone pirates are so inevitable.

> ❷ YARR, WE BE HAVING YOUR YOGA MAT AND BE WANTING NO LESS THAN EIGHT PIECES O' GOLD FOR IT.

❸ Bitcoins.* Pieces of eight are so last century.

. . . .

I wonder if the drones will be on zero-hour contracts?

. . . .

Apparently it's been a real success. The home targeted for delivery was utterly destroyed.

. . . .

What has Santa got to say about all this? They're going to put him out of a job.

. . . .

❶ What about the impact on birds?

❷ Birds have never been very good at delivering packages, they'll be fine. I'm more worried about postmen.

. . . .

As someone with a drone landing pad (back garden) and a postie who can't be arsed to shut the gate, I say great news.

_____

* Online currency, difficult to use in vending machines.

5
My Family and
Other Animals

....

Family is, of course, the most important thing in the world to many people. This is why BBC3 continues to show the same 12 episodes of *Family Guy* on continuous loop and BBC1 carried on making *My Family* for years, even though it was terrible. Guardianistas love their families as much as anyone else – providing they put the rubbish in the correct bin for recycling, don't mess too much with the thermostat and let them watch *Family Guy* before bedtime. Every family has its own traditions, its own values, and its own way of embarrassing its children, and our comments give a lovely snapshot into a weird world of Sunday dinners and ethical Christmases.

Modern Family Traditions

....

We enjoy Japanese animated films, and once a month
we dress up as Victorians and go out for the day.
Absolutely true.

....

In my house we have many fine traditions. My favourite
takes place on Saturday afternoons: Arabella and
Hannibal, my two children, will often sit together and see
who can remember the most lines from *Hamlet*. I look
on, macchiato in hand, and gently chide them when they
become too competitive, or when they start trying to
sneak in quotations from *King Lear*, the cheeky devils!

....

We eat a meal together seven days a week, love folk
music and go on two holidays a year, one of which
is always in the UK. Next: a week in the Highlands,
camping, hiking, whisky and generally trying to get
the kids not to stab each other. The other holiday is to
places like Zambia, Indonesia, Madagascar – the kids
love it that much that they put up with the UK bit.

Every summer, weather permitting, her outdoors and I attend a nice and secluded meadow near Welham Green and indulge in some very good alfresco sex; hardly a family tradition but then again we are not a typical family . . . god forbid.

....

I have never seen *Outnumbered*. I don't have time to watch TV as I am too busy looking after my kids.

....

In our family there is no such thing as 'my money'. We are a unit, and so it is 'our money'.

Parenting
....

I can't believe the writer of this article actually used the word 'parenting'. Parent is a noun not a verb.*

....

_____
* Damn. Can we apologise for the title of this section?

I detested childhood, until I discovered what the degradations of adulthood in a contemporary neoliberal society entailed. Now I just hate life altogether.

. . . .

Re. Moving your family to a new town for school

❶ Research before you move, particularly when you are moving to a rural area with limited resources. We've had an influx of people moving to our area in recent years, they spend half their time moaning there is no Waitrose and that the pub serves pork pies rather than rocket salad.

❷ No Waitrose?!

. . . .

I did a Forest School course at the weekend. UK kids are the unhappiest in Europe and the only antidote is a couple of hours a week being driven to some woodland and told to play with mud.

. . . .

Re: Family dinners

Ready-meals, ready-made lifestyles, ready-made outlook, ready-made sentiments. Pretty soon, the only thing we'll be capable of *making* is a mess of our lives.

❶ My dad worked hard to bring home the bacon.

          ❷ Bacon? Isn't that 'dietary abuse'? Children
          have been taken into care for less.

         ❸ Hmmm, I'm not even sure about the 'bring home'
         bit. Isn't home delivery more ecologically sound?

. . . .

Whenever someone asks, 'Does your wife work?', I say,
'All the time, but she's not earning any money.'

. . . .

Re: Lily Allen claiming babies are boring

Who thought babies were meant to be a thrilling leisure
activity? Tell her to buy a skateboard.

. . . .

My baby hasn't even got a Twitter account yet, so we've
no idea when he needs changing or wants feeding.
Sometimes we'll be at a party all night long and he
won't even send an IM on Facebook to let us know how
he is. Selfish little sod.

. . . .

❶ Here in the US eating freeze-dried placenta is becoming popular. Not my cup of tea though.

❷ Where do you think Tesco's burgers come from, since the horsemeat scandal?

. . . .

Re: Eating the placenta after giving birth

My wife and I ate it with garlic, salt and pepper with perhaps just some red pepper and courgette. No, not washed down by a nice Chianti. We live in the Languedoc, after all. For the record, she recovered from the (natural, home) birth in record time and attributes it to the celebratory dinner.

. . . .

First two weeks of paternity leave: 'This is the most amazing thing in the world! Babies are amazing!' Next ten weeks: 'Move or . . . do something!'

Name That Baby
. . . .

I'd rather have Peyton, Edward or Alfonso than David, Ian or Nigel. Don't even try to mention Boris.

Overheard in a supermarket, a mother yelling at a child: 'Stop that now, our Reebok.' REEBOK? Definitely a case needing the Pope's intervention.

. . . .

Parents should not be allowed to buy books called 'Baby Names'. They forget that they are not naming a cute little baby; they are naming someone who they hope will become a confident happy 30-year-old. Called Sonny, or Fifi. The books should be called 'Person-who-will-be-choosing-your-retirement-home Names'.

. . . .

When I moved to Oz 30-odd years ago, I met a couple who had named their daughter 'Lamorna'.
I mentioned that the only Lamorna that I knew about was Lamorna Cove in Cornwall. The lady blushed and said, 'It was a beautiful beach . . . and there was nobody around!'

. . . .

❶ There seems to be a trend towards naming a child after the place where she or he was conceived. For instance, I know of a Coimbra, a Venezia, a Pula – though not, unless someone is keeping quiet about it, a BackseatofaHillmanMinx.

❷ I used to have a Hillman Minx and take it from me conception would have been a miracle.

. . . .

❶ Before you commit to naming a child, you should say the name over and over. The problem with the name Noah is it just isn't pleasant 'in the mouth' – when saying it, the face naturally forms into an expression of distaste.

❷ Trying to think about names that are pleasurable in the mouth . . . Horatio?

❸ I tried doing this with my son Candyman,* it did not end well.

. . . .

---

* Reference to early 90s horror film about a hook-handed bogeyman who appeared when you said his name three times. Bloody terrifying.

I waited my whole life (to this point) to name a son after my father Alfred. For most of this time 'Alfie' or 'Alf' has been deeply unfashionable, which was much to my liking. Imagine my horror when my lazy breeding schedule coincided with a million other Alfies, leaving me to explain that I don't watch *EastEnders* to a disbelieving public.

. . . .

I called my children Nye (short for Aneurin, after Bevan) and Rosa (after Luxembourg and Parks). They have only come across two others in their lives with the same names.

. . . Go Together Like a Horse and Carriage?

. . . .

Re: Should you wear an engagement ring?

I find engaged people never shut up about it, so a physical display is rarely needed.

. . . .

Re: The cost of wedding dresses

If you get divorced and then get married again in the same dress it becomes much better value.

We went to the Register Office in our ordinary clothes,
bought in the sales. No rings. Same contract.

. . . .

I had a completely green, eco, carbon-free wedding:
I didn't have one.

. . . .

Who the hell would marry *anyone* called Freddie?

I Wish It Could Be Christmas Every Day

. . . .

I always felt that Christmas was meant to teach children
how to cope with disappointment and boredom.

. . . .

On Christmas Day I expect home cooking at its best.
Only the Christmas pudding is bought ready-made. I am
actually doing wild boar this year.

. . . .

❶ Getting completely soused as a family on vast quantities of wines, beers and spirits is a tradition I for one would keep. Anything else is essentially superfluous.

❷ Oh yes, the joys of substance abuse . . .

. . . .

From the age of about seven my younger brother used to dress up as the art-loving nun, Sister Wendy, to distribute the gifts on Christmas morning. He was too young to make a convincing Father Christmas and that was our next best bet. It didn't seem strange at the time.

. . . .

We always have a HUGE bottle of full-sugar Ribena, as a treat.

. . . .

We watch no television at Christmas, none at all. We consider this a great bonus.

My Animals and Other Family

The only person everyone in my family likes is the dog.

While I was driving along this morning my two-year-old boy took the opportunity to point out: 'Dad . . . Hedgehogs don't talk.' He's right. Weird, but right.

❶ I was watching a hedgehog and a rat fighting in the garden over a bit of bread . . . it went on for ages but the hedgehog eventually won on points.

❷ I'm not surprised. You could never call them spineless.

❸ I think the rat probably felt a bit of a prick, come the end.

It's illegal to keep monkeys as pets, and yet it's OK to elect one as mayor of London?

....

The bunny can be eaten if Cara falls on hard times. I would suggest a light red wine, with mushroom and cream sauce.

....

I gave my dog *Fifty Shades of Grey** on his Kindle for Christmas, and as soon as I can free myself from these dog leads, I'm going right ahead and deleting it.

....

As a husband, father of two daughters and servant of a cat, I have a dog to maintain some sense of ego and authority. It's nice to be admired and adored.

....

Pieces of eight . . . or two fours will do.

---

* *Fifty Shades of Grey*: mucky book, responsible for surge in sales of handcuffs and whips and the fact you can genuinely now buy grey ties in Anne Summers.

You should always keep more than one fish so that they can communicate:* 'Look at that rock.' 'What's a rock?' 'Why do you ask?' 'Ask what?' 'Look at that rock . . .'

. . . .

If goldfish were unhappy they'd cry. If they cried there would be more water in the bowl in the morning not the same amount. Ergo, fish are quite OK with things.

. . . .

My little girl's hamster is a bit like Doctor Who – he has a habit of dying and coming back younger.[†]

. . . .

Re: The popularity of cat videos

Cats are archetypal Tories. They dislike everything that doesn't directly contribute to their own comfort; hate change; treat the rest of the world with contempt and expect to be waited on hand and foot . . .

---

* Goldfish, of course, famously have short memories, and thus make excellent pets for those friends we all have who insist on telling the same stories over and over. If you don't know anyone like this, then I'm afraid it's probably you.

[†] Anyone currently getting ready to email in pointing out that the Doctor doesn't ALWAYS get younger, can you take a moment to think long and hard about your life? Thanks.

They are slowly taking over the world. First your chair and sofa, then your bed, then your laundry, then the space between you and your computer, your food and/or water, then your husband or wife or child or any nice strangers that are foolish enough to feed or give them treats, and now infiltrating the internet in view of world domination.

The Nanny State

....

Re: Buggy with built-in phone charger

Well, you wouldn't want your battery to go flat and have to interact with your child, would you?

. . . .

Re: What would happen if grandparents refused to babysit?

Sales of Werther's Original* would skyrocket, the *Gardener's Question Time* switchboard would have to take on more staff, and queues at Waitrose checkouts during working hours would double in length.

. . . .

---

* Werther's Original: Tasty caramel sweet. Many OAPs have found they can exist on a permanent diet of these.

My niece calls Thomas the Tank Engine 'Hummus the Tank Engine'.

. . . .

My son has cost me a fortune with his chronic Lego addiction. It is time to ban this plastic brick filth.

. . . .

Re: Vintage *Star Wars* toys selling for £18,000

I have over sixty *Star Wars* figures from the late 70s and early 80s collected by my youngest son. He has forgotten all about them. Shall I tell him? I love him dearly but . . . sod it. I have other sons.

. . . .

Re: Lego *Doctor Who* sets

❶ It's quite possible that the Lego Danny Pink* will have more personality than the real one.

❷ John Barrowman's figure will literally be made out of ham.

. . . .

---

* Danny Pink: Boring minor character in *Doctor Who*. Became the world's most disappointing cyberman.

I buy tatty old Sindy* and Barbie dolls from charity shops and boot sales, and give them new hair and faces and clothes. The ones with missing limbs get biomechanical-style prostheses. I'm going to start selling them soon, once I've mastered the art, but in the interim my house is cluttered with doll parts. It's brilliant. I've never felt so goth.

. . . .

Re: Why Disney's *Frozen* toys will be the big thing this Christmas

Really? As a 32-year-old bloke I was hoping for my regularly scheduled pack of socks, tangerines and bottle of single malt.

---

* Sindy: Barbie's dowdy English cousin.

6
The Hitchhiker's Guide
to Planet Earth

....

Guardian readers are a well-travelled lot, although they're stereotypically associated with the ski slope or Polly Toynbee's Tuscan villa. (FACT: It's a myth that Polly has a villa in Tuscany and she is constantly bewildered by the sarcastic references to it that occur in the comments below her articles. Besides, everyone knows Umbria is much nicer.) From gap yahs to package holidays, home and abroad, *Guardian* readers have traversed the world, and are only too happy to share their experiences.

Across the Pond

Las Vegas is unspeakably vulgar. Why would anyone want to sully their spirituality by associating with it?

I see by your driving plans that you are skipping the real Florida. It would appear that all you want to do is get to Miami. Travelling Mercies then. Peace out.

What's with all the San Francisco loving in the *Guardian* today? I know it's a big place, but there's plenty of stuff going on in Cirencester at the moment.

American Craft Beer is a world beater. Are you listening, CAMRA?*

---

* The Campaign for Real Ale: a British organisation dedicated to combating gassy cheap lager and the promotion of proper craft beers, alongside lengthy facial hair and fishing hats.

'Do You Ski?'

....

Re: Combined skiing and yoga holidays (costing £400)

99% of the world lives on less than £400 a week. Next time do yoga in your front room and send the £400 to a charity.

....

I love the juxtaposition of articles in this paper decrying the lack of social mobility in society while giving guides to skiing in Val d'Isère.

....

Re: The glass-bottomed viewing platform at the top of a French mountain

❶ I am giddy and feel nauseous just looking at the photos. I think I'm slipping from my chair and the floor seems a long way off . . . Noooooo . . .

      ❷ Maybe you should give up your swivel chair.

❸ After a Ryanair flight to Lyon, getting into a glass box 1000 metres up will feel quite comforting.

....

Great: the Pyrenees are forgotten again!

Leaving on a Jet Plane . . .

....

Airline employees were so much more agreeable back when they were all drunk.

Flying with easyJet has scarred me for life.

. . . .

❶ All Ghana needs now is a Ryanair route.

> ❷ Which will fly to Togo and you'll have get
> a bus from there.

. . . .

Why the hell would you fly on a budget airline in the first
place? You sacrificed any claims to a decent flight the
minute you bought the ticket.

. . . .

Re: Things that should be banned on flights

I'd ban . . . Babies and toddlers (unless heavily dosed),
the significantly overweight, people with those annoying
voices that echo round the plane so that you can hear
their whole conversation from miles away, people
with annoying laughs, Americans, and smug weekend
newspaper columnists.

. . . .

I don't think my old dad would have been too impressed with this 'nightmare' journey out of Italy. He came home from Rome in the bomb bay of a malfunctioning Lancaster bomber in 1945, with a circle marked on the floor instead of a seat and an emergency landing to deliver him from five years of fighting. I suppose all nightmares are relative.

Brits Abroad

....

I won't forget drinking sacrificial-deer blood mixed with rice wine on Buddhist New Year with a family in Laos, while a group of 'Brits Abroad' bobbed past in inflatables on the Mekong singing 'Don't Look Back in Anger'.

....

As a 31-year-old, I cannot go on a Club 18–30 holiday – an argument for suing them for discrimination?

....

Amsterdam is hell on earth. Total anarchy. Millions of near-naked women, on bicycles. I will not return.

....

Whereabouts in Tuscany is Butlins? I can't see it on any maps.

. . . .

Re: How to have a budget holiday in Italy

I live in Siena and think tourists already have a very good idea of how to do things on the cheap. Witness the people with their supermarket bags having picnics in Piazza del Campo, or sharing one salad or plate of pasta in a restaurant. The ultimate way to save money is to stay at home and look at it on the internet!

. . . .

Re: Beer-tasting holidays in Tuscany

Idiotic. On a par with the Americans I met in Paris looking for Mexican food.

. . . .

Re: Italian resorts banning trashy souvenirs

This is seriously going to affect my collection of memorabilia with Michelangelo's *David*'s member on it.

. . . .

I had the bus journey from hell to an obscure suburb of Rome to do a one-day zumba qualification. I would have paid a lot to have not suffered the anxiety of that.

. . . .

Ibiza would be my idea of purgatory. Pointless clubbing with gyrating exhibitionists and pounding noise. Hedonism without any of the actual pleasures.

. . . .

If you want to re-create Ibiza at home just flush loads of money down the toilet while taking lots of drugs. I mean, come on, the main attraction of the island is watching the sun rise? You can do that anywhere!

. . . .

Re: Increasing tourism in Budapest

Another authentic city district ruined.

. . . .

French wines are toxic, unless they are 'natural'. Don't buy wine unless it is from the emerging 'natural-wine' movement.

. . . .

Ah, nothing ruins a magical isolated paradise like pointing them all out on the front page of the *Guardian*. 'Honey, I've read about an amazing isolated beach in Indonesia' . . . Two years down the line, 'Where did all of these gap-year students come from?'

. . . .

Frankly, 'paradise' for me would be being able to do something constructive and socially useful.

. . . .

Sickeningly ironic that so many of these tips about 'paradise' involve long flights, which of course contribute so directly to climate change and planet death. Perhaps this article should be renamed 'The Deniers' Guide to Selfish Holidays'?

. . . .

Re: Road trip across Canada

These 'road-trip' articles clash horribly with the *Guardian*'s otherwise laudable stance on selfish and wasteful use of precious fossil fuels.

. . . .

Re: Seasickness

❶ Hi, Gordon Brown here (not that one). I've never been seasick; at times the whole crew was throwing up. Sometimes it was just me and the skipper who weren't sick; sometimes just me.

> ❷ Are you *sure* you're not 'the' Gordon Brown? Would put a whole different meaning on your post if you were . . .

. . . .

Re: Goa's quest for a better class of tourist

They should change the name to 'Goaway'.

. . . .

There's only one thing spoiling Thailand, and that's the foreigners there.

. . . .

Re: The Great Wall of China

Great? Longest wall in the world and not a single cash machine!

. . . .

South Korean pop music is the best argument I've heard for the state of North Korea.

Hi-De-Hi Campers – Holidaying at Home

....

❶ Let's show the French that British food is better than it's painted.

❷ Painted? What next?

....

Re: Life sentences for criminals

❶ Hang them. Prison would be a life of holiday!

❷ Were you taken to Butlins as a child too?

❸ Butlins in Minehead? Five minutes of that and they will voluntarily drown themselves.

....

I would rather forgo a holiday than go to Butlins.

....

I thought steak was the choice of the unambitious – you know, like consistency, chinos, urban 4×4s and holidays at Center Parcs.

. . . .

I have only ever sent food back twice in my life. Both at Center Parcs.

. . . .

Anywhere that describes itself as 'open for business' is not where I want to go for a holiday, thank you very much.

. . . .

Re: Holidays in the South West of England

It looks lovely down there. Like going to Yorkshire, but not quite as good.

. . . .

Re: Celebrity holiday destinations

I notice that no one admits to a week in Skegness.

. . . .

I couldn't think of anything more ghastly than an Ibiza holiday, but Haworth [in Yorkshire] is a tremendous experience.

. . . .

Why spend a day by some wet beach when you can book your holiday when it's quiet and jet off to France or Spain instead for two weeks? And everything doesn't shut early.

. . . .

Your kids will hate adventure holidays just as much as you did. My parents dragged us up-hill-and-down-bog and have left me enjoying nature only when it is presented to me by the BBC in the comfort of my living room.

. . . .

Bee stings in unmentionable places, soggy ice-cream, rows and vomiting in the back of a Hillman Imp . . . You can keep it, quite frankly. I'd rather stay at home and do my own thing these days.

The Hitchhiker's Guide to Other Planets

....

Phallic-shaped rockets are in themselves sexist. This needs to be addressed.

....

Mars belongs to men – you don't see us trying to go to Venus, do you?

....

As long as they can grow tea and fly regular refuelling missions carrying Hobnobs, British people can survive on Mars.

....

Re: 'Dwarf planets'

Don't you mean 'planet of small stature'?

The Great Outdoors

....

❶ As I waited to drive into work early one morning, I watched a fox play around on the nearby grass, only to have it jump onto the bonnet of my car. After looking at me for a few seconds it jumped off, and ran away. Absolutely made my day.

❷ Supposedly they also jump over lazy dogs a lot. People are always writing about it.

....

Re: Walking holidays in France

You'd like walking a lot less if you'd read about Napoleon's 1812 retreat from Moscow.

....

Re: Wild swimming recommendations

Good god man keep it to yourself! I know of quite a few really good spots in the Lakes that I won't be mentioning. Fortunately they are very rarely frequented, long may they stay that way!

....

You do all know that anywhere else in the world this would just be called 'swimming'?

. . . .

❶ Anyone willing to hike naked in Northern Scotland has balls.

        ❷ Not during midge season they don't.

. . . .

Nothing would induce me to use a commercial campsite. Nothing.

. . . .

Re: Best campsites in Britain

❶ They all look infested with children. A campsite with noisy children around is called a town.

        ❷ Welcome to the miserable git thread.

. . . .

I do a lot of guerrilla winter camping when I don't quite make it home from Wetherspoon's steak club night.

That's probably the first time I've read the word 'stunning' in the same sentence as 'Isle of Sheppey'. At least, as a compliment.

All the Fun of the Fair

···

Re: Life-sized 'replica' helter-skelter

Isn't a 'replica helter-skelter' just a helter-skelter?

·································

Re: Harry Potter studio tour in Watford

Sounds great, but . . . Watford? No.

·································

We don't need historical theme parks, Britain basically already is one.

·································

Mock Walt Disney all you like, but Disneyland is the only place in the LA area with a functioning public transport system.

·································

Re: Napoleon theme park proposed in France

I can't believe the French would go for this, but if they do, why don't they call it 'Napoleon Bonapark'?

. . . .

Re: Reopening of Margate's classic 'Dreamland' theme park

The Kent coast really does this 50s revival well. That's why UKIP is so popular there.

. . . .

❶ Skegness' Fantasy Island does seven-day passes for those staying the week in the resort. Does anyone know if Margate's Dreamland does similar?

❷ Margate is not a place anybody would want to stay in for a week.

7
A Guide to Great Britain and Northern Ireland

··

You can always rely on the British for pathological and completely ungrounded hatred for largely blameless parts of their country. You'll be hard pushed to find a Scouser with a nice word to say on Manchester; a Yorkshireman would rather walk through fire than be complimentary about Lancashire; whereas the only thing a Lancastrian hates more than a Londoner is, well, a Yorkshireman. Cornwall and Yorkshire claim to be 'God's own country', which suggests that if nothing else God is fond of a cream tea, although which way round should he do the cream and the jam? Cornishmen and their Devonshire neighbours have come to blows over this for years, while a resident of North London will moan about anyone born above the Watford Gap, but would still rather venture past the Midlands than go south of the river. Given all this, it's astonishing most Brits are able to leave their own street, so convinced are we that the rest of the country is a bit disappointing.

Aberdeen

Aberdeen is just like Hawaii crossed with Switzerland, combining the cultural sophistication of, say, Paris, New York and Verbier.

. . . .

Ashby-de-la-Zouch

We have a biscuit factory, a soap factory, an outdoor swimming pool, a market and a pub with a stuffed grizzly bear. What we don't have though is Ashby Canal, but a pub with a bear is not to be sniffed at.

. . . .

Bedford

I'm so glad I live so, so, so far away from Bedfordshire – it sounds pish.

. . . .

Belfast

A bit like Mogadishu, without the sun.

. . . .

Birmingham

It's arguably one of the most hideous city centres I've ever seen. One fancy, expensive library cannot possibly redeem the festival of ugliness that is Birmingham city centre.

. . . .

Bracknell

'The man who's tired of Bracknell is tired of life.' Not sure about that one.

. . . .

Brighton

Pebbly beach. Not terribly beautiful. Preferred Whitby.

. . . .

Brighton

I just don't get the 'seaside', wherever it is. Unless Brighton feels it's being ironic, it is just so passé. Mountains and lakes for me.

. . . .

Bristol

Am I understanding this correctly – they're going to put a giant inflatable water slide right smack on the road????? And people are actually hailing this as genius????? It looks unseemly and is such a stupid thing to do. Bristol is not a kids' playhouse. Everybody will become obese. What harm is there in plain old walking? None.

. . . .

Bristol

Can the council ban hippies? Bristol is inundated with them. Like pigeons.

. . . .

Bristol

All this beauty, all built on the slave trade.

. . . .

Canvey Island

What happens below sea level stays below sea level.

. . . .

Carlisle

It's only 25 miles from Cockermouth and it has a good Marks & Spencer.

. . . .

Carlisle

I've only been through Carlisle while hitching so know only two things about the place: it's very close to the water table and it is a mecca for plasterers.

. . . .

The Channel Islands

❶ Re: The best islands in the UK. As a Jerseyman, I don't care where we come in the list so long as we are higher than Guernsey.

❷ As a Guernseyman I'm not sure I'd have Jersey on a Top-10 islands and islets of the Channel Islands, let alone Top 10 of the UK(ish).

. . . .

Chesterfield

Surprised no one has mentioned the fact that the roundabouts in Chesterfield are the single worst in the entire country.

Cornwall

It's like the Florida Keys without the sunshine: you get there and it's grey, pebbledashed houses and no cheer whatsoever. There's potential aplenty, but without effort Cornwall will always be Leonard Cohen masquerading as a Beach Boys song.

. . . .

Croydon

Re: Survey of the best places to live in Britain. How on earth did Croydon do so well in this survey?

. . . .

Devon

Along with Scottish Independence can we vote to get rid of Devon? But this time can we cut it off from the rest of Britain and let it float out to sea?

. . . .

Dorset

Culture in North Dorset? Only the Larmer Tree Music Festival could be described as culture and most of that is in Wiltshire.

. . . .

Dublin

Drink to forget.

. . . .

East Ham

FACT: All places with 'Ham' in the name tend to have residents that live longer including – unfortunately – Buckingham Palace.

. . . .

Essex

Best thing about Brentwood? The lido and that closed years ago.

. . . .

Glamorgan

Anywhere west of West Cross is OK, but avoid Swansea at all costs; it makes Chernobyl look like Monaco.

. . . .

Glasgow

Stop dreaming, boys, the happiest city is always Glasgow! Why? Because we are not in Edinburgh, that is why!

. . . .

Glossop

From the many times I've driven through it, I assumed it was just a damp grey disappointment of a town built around a permanent traffic jam.

. . . .

Harrogate

Main Attraction: Betty's Cafe . . . Better standard of life . . . Betty's tea cakes are five times as good as your southern tea cakes.

. . . .

Hounslow

Hounslow, can you go?

. . . .

Leeds

LSD and a couple of Es.

. . . .

Leicester

No amount of dead Plantagenets would ever entice me back to Leicester.

Liverpool

Who'd live in a Scouse like this?

. . . .

Liverpool

Liver-poo.

. . . .

London

Who'd want to live in Southampton rather than Notting Hill, Mayfair, Knightsbridge, Chelsea, Hampstead, Camden, Brixton, Whitechapel or Soho? No one I know.

. . . .

London

I'd die of boredom and enforced celibacy anywhere other than East London. My only worry is the pace of gentrification round here. It's in danger of losing its edge.

. . . .

London

The countryside? Yes, I love it and visit often, but to live? No, thanks. My villages are Dulwich, Blackheath and Barnes. If I decide to go oop north, Highgate will do me.

[131]

London

'In praise of Peckham'? Good luck with that.

. . . .

London

Move to New Cross? I'd rather take a wire brush to my scrotum.

. . . .

London

The World is your Oyster Card.

. . . .

Luton

Can Luton please become 'Lutonshire' and thus stop blighting the reputation of the otherwise gorgeous county of Bedfordshire?

. . . .

Manchester

No one wants to go there. I hear it's cold, violent and lacks even the basics – like sushi and decent tapas.

. . . .

Manchester

They paved paradise and put up a parking lot.

. . . .

Milton Keynes

You'll like it, in a roundabout way.

. . . .

Morecambe

Very Wise.

. . . .

Newcastle

Newcastle is one of the greatest places in Britain.
Comparing it to London is like comparing ice-cream to
horse manure.

. . . .

Newcastle

Drink till you puke, eat a kebab, then punch a policeman
and nick his horse.

. . . .

Norfolk

Constant nose-to-tail traffic, sugarbeet smells, that accent, a lot of God Shops, expensive housing, no social housing, full of tourists, no IKEA and worst of all, more Wetherspoons than any other county.

. . . .

The North

I was born in Lancashire and spent five years in Yorkshire at university and afterwards. I'm truly torn as to where my loyalties lie, but at least I'm not from Down South.

. . . .

The North

Do not publish articles about places north of Stoke – people will start moving up here and we don't want that, do we?

. . . .

Nottingham

Nottingham. Drink till you puke, eat a kebab, then punch a policeman.

. . . .

Plymouth

Being cut off from the rest of the country twice a year merely adds to our unique charm.

. . . .

Ramsbottom

If the town is as boring as [hometown band] Elbow I'm not going near it.

. . . .

Scunthorpe

Ignored by search engines with high moral standards.

. . . .

Southend

If you think this is shit, you've clearly never been to Tilbury.

. . . .

The Isle of Skye

I bet the nearest M&S food department is, like, a hundred miles away.

. . . .

Solihull

Solihull is a classic 'actually' town, as in: 'Are you from Birmingham?' 'No, Solihull actually', although then topped by 'Are you from Solihull?' 'No, Knowle actually', and so on as you work your way out to ever-posher Warwickshire villages . . .

. . . .

The South

Why would anybody want to live in the South East of England? It's ghastly!

. . . .

Stockport

I once said to my son that when I picture Stockport, I always think it's raining there. He replied, 'It's the tears of the people.'

. . . .

Watford

Watfor?

. . . .

Wales

I particularly like the way that 'Cymru' is advertised as soon as you go anywhere west of London. It does give Wales that sort of mythical, mystic, old-worldly dimensional quality that seems to be lacking in Watford.

....

Wallsend

The blight at the end of the tunnel.

....

Wokingham

❶ It pisses me off that everyone is saying that Wokingham is a boring place. The gay scene is awesome there and it must have more S&M clubs per head of population than anywhere else in Britain. Why was that not reported?

❷ Congratulations on whipping up enthusiasm for Wokingham.

....

Worcester

Not as saucy as you'd think.

....

Yorkshire

Only two good things to come out of Yorkshire: Alan Bennett and the road into Lancashire.

. . . .

York

Old York. (I ♥ OY)

8
Now That's What
I Call Culture

··

The *Guardian*'s cultural community is an odd beast. On the one hand we have some of the best music and film criticism going and our readers reflect this – they are knowledgeable, obsessive, passionate and will argue, recommend or write daft puns at the drop of a hat. We also have a lively and smart arts readership who pitch in with their views on the latest classical music, opera and theatre; and of course we live in a world of endless popcorn movies and reality TV – indeed our *X-Factor* and *Apprentice* live blogs are the stuff of internet legend. These three communities, it has to be said, tend not to rub along all that well: the arty crowd look down on the pop culture lot, the pop culture lot look down on the reality TV lot, the reality TV lot look down on reality TV contestants, and Simon Cowell looks down on all of them, rubbing his hands and cackling.

Now That's What I Call Festivals

....

Re: 2014 Glastonbury line-up

❶ A good gauge of how old you've become can be gleaned by counting the number of bands that you are familiar with appearing at Glastonbury. This year's list confirms that I must be at least 120 years old.

❷ The line-up in no way interests or excites me, apart from one or two acts. Me? I'll be running around the stone circle, nude, covering up my genitals with a mandolin.

The best Glastonbury was 2005: I didn't bring wellingtons, never mind a coat, so I went barefoot for the whole weekend. It was liberating.

....

I don't want to be a killjoy on this subject, but today's youth gather in even bigger groups than we did back in the 1960s/1970s. The emissions of methane and other toxic gasses from the human body help to destroy the ozone layer.

....

South by South West Festival? Where advertising and the best of corporate America meets what's left of rock 'n' roll.

Now That's What I Call Boybands to Britpop
....

The success of One Direction shows why teenage girls should not be allowed money.

....

Q: What's blue and can't sing?
A: Blue.*

————————
* Blue: boyband. Lovely voices, no braincells.

Re: Forgotten boybands

Anyone remember Let Loose?*

❷ Was that a laxative?

. . . .

❶ I'm still shocked by my recent discovery that 5ive
now have only four members.

❷ Austerity.

. . . .

Re: Article that stated, 'The intensity of support for Harry
Styles and Co. demands I crown them [One Direction] the best
[boyband] of all time.'

Glad this writer wasn't at the Nuremberg Rallies.

. . . .

Saying One Direction is 'the best boyband ever' is like
saying chlamydia is the best STD ever.

. . . .

I was into battle rap before it got commercial.

---

* Let Loose: 90s boyband, played their own instruments, were
'Crazy For You'.

I, personally, will NEVER take trash like hip hop seriously. Just leave me with talented artists of quality: the likes of Dizzy, John Coltrane, Clifford Brown, Thelonious Monk and Sarah Vaughan.

....

Re: 2Pac brought back to life as a hologram

Imagine what could be done in ballet! A new version of *The Rite of Spring* as choreographed by Pina Bausch, with the young Pina in the main role, surrounded by real dancers . . .

....

The only time P. Diddy* has been relevant is when Nas dressed up in some sort of homage to him in his *Hate Me Now* video. Diddy has never been relevant.

....

Re: The joy of pop music

Has the writer never heard, or come across, any classical music (Bach, Mozart, Beethoven, Brahms, John Tavener, Messiaen, Gibbons, Byrd, Victoria, Purcell?). Popular stuff's OK for switch-off or disco-dancing times, but you can draw so much more from the classical canon!

---

* P Diddy: rapper, known variously as Puff Daddy, Puffy and Diddy. Actual name is Sean.

You should have bought the albums on vinyl.
Remastering is vandalism.

. . . .

Well, as long as the tour is called that, I won't be buying
a ticket. It's a ruddy disgrace. Further, if the weather's
nice tomorrow I'll be smashing all my Beyoncé CDs in
the garden with a toffee hammer.

. . . .

'Popular chart music' is frequently (though not
exclusively) a deliberately narrow selection chosen by
career philistine accountants and broadcast editors
for the benefit of the shareholders, and is therefore
obviously not in any way representative of the wonder,
beauty and power of music.

. . . .

Three chords and Beatles rehashes do not really make
a pop movement.

---

* Britpop: 90s musical movement that celebrated the best bands
of the 60s and 70s by sounding exactly the same as them.

Can all the people on this forum claiming that 'Disco 2000' by Pulp is a better song than 'Crazy in Love' please link to photographs of themselves. I have a mental picture of what you look like, but I'd like to see if I am right or not.

. . . .

Re: Pulp's 'Common People' voted favourite Britpop anthem

❶ Well, although as an award it's right up there with being 'Least bad British Leyland designed and built car', it's certainly deserved.

❷ I nominate the Triumph Dolomite Sprint for that accolade.

. . . .

❶ Does anybody know if Louise Wener from Sleeper is still gorgeous?

❷ From what I remember of interviews with her, I suspect she still thinks so.

. . . .

No one has ever written a song as good as 'Disco Down' by Shed Seven.*

· ·

Re: Britpop

A stinking cesspit of mediocrity and vile characters wallowing in a miasma of regressive banality with not an original idea among them, I hope they all rot in hell. Especially the cheese-maker from Blur.

Now That's What I Call Strictly Britain's Got the Talent Idol Factor

· ·

Re: *The X Factor*

Horrible, horrible show. I would shoot my own children if they liked this.

· ·

People are hungry for a real talent show with writer/ musicians showcasing their works. Singers that do not write/play are of little interest to me, like a waiter presenting the chef's craft.

---

* Shed Seven: unjustly overlooked indie band, though not as overlooked as Sheds One to Six.

First a massive plane crash, then all that NSA bollocks, and now this? Thanks for ruining my Tuesday, world!

....

I think the difference between *X-Factor* judges and the coalition government is that no matter how dislikeable the judges may come across, they do have some experience and knowledge of the things they're talking about.

....

I honestly believe Simon Cowell is a psychopath. He has about as much empathy as a Nazi dentist.

....

I hate the way *X Factor* has turned the Christmas number one into a boring over-commercialised piece of forgettable crap. I miss the good old days of real musicians like Spice Girls and Westlife.

....

It is increasingly clear that [*X-Factor* winner] Matt Cardle's hat is being used to pass on messages from aliens.

Now That's What I Call Christmas

Sainsbury's was playing a load of 1940s Christmas stuff this week. It was like grocery shopping in Fallout 3.*

To make a blow for culture, could the *Guardian* put together a CD (or download) of Solstice music that is guaranteed to be free of sectarian references?

While I am normally very tolerant, 'Mistletoe and Wine' makes me think religious persecution isn't always a bad thing.

Re: iPods

This toy certainly hasn't changed the way I listen to music – on a comfy sofa with a glass of single malt and a high-end hi-fi system, not on a bus with poncy earbuds and an MP3 compressed to within an inch of its life.

---

* Fallout 3: Post-apocalyptic computer game.

Now That's What I Call The Beatles

···

Re: Picture of the Beatles having a pillow fight

❶ I think Ringo* ruins it.

❷ I agree. Ringo has not got the technical pillowsmanship of the others. That's what held them back in those early days. Pete Best was a much better pillow fighter. Who knows how good they could have been with cushion in hand if he'd stayed around?

·································

Did you know that Beatlemania is an anagram of braindead cretinous fandom? True story.

Now That's What I Call Telly

···

Downton Abbey, or as the Tories like to call it, 'a fly-on-the-wall documentary'.

·································

---

* Ringo Starr: voice of Thomas the Tank Engine, not even the best drummer in the Beatles.

Downton Abbey has done great service to Britain. By keeping Cameron and Osborne glued to the screen each week (under the impression they are watching grandfather's home movies) it ensures one day a week when the risk of their meddling is reduced.

....

Every day, I'm glad I don't have a TV.

....

Re: *Homeland*

Have to admit to being slightly ashamed of myself for watching something that has its origins in an Israeli series though. Is Channel 4 indirectly subsidising Israel?

....

After seeing a few episodes of *My Family* my desire to see anything made by British TV on the British family has shrivelled up and died.

....

Re: 'My favourite show is *Top Gear*.'

Great, you're a Tory and petrolhead that sees consumerist ownership as an extension of your male virility then.

❶ Jeremy Paxman is a god.

    ❷ A rather terrifying Old Testament one, but yes.

. . . .

University Challenge is pretty much the only thing on TV that's worth watching.

. . . .

I suggest you all get a copy of Dennis Potter's *Singing Detective* and watch it up to Joanne Whalley's immortal line (no spoiler here) and the dance breakout to 'Dem Bones'. Then consider whether all these American shows you seem to think are so great are really worth the inordinate amount of hours you have to invest, when you can just replay that.

. . . .

Re: *The Golden Girls*

Don't you wish your girlfriend was hot like Bea?

. . . .

Re: *Doctor Who*

❶ I will never forget the Doctor's and Captain Jack's kiss in the first reboot series. Absolutely breathtaking, not only for the fact that it was broadcast at all, but for the fact that here we have two men sufficiently comfortable with themselves that they can actually snog on screen!

❷ If the Doctor is kissing *anyone* then it's not *The Doctor*. Why not freshen it up by getting rid of the TARDIS, the Doctor, the companions, and all references to science fiction; and adding five male comedians plus Jenny Eclair* to discuss in a light-hearted manner the issues of the day?

. . . .

I had a choice between watching *Mrs Brown's Boys* and hammering rusty nails into my balls. Has anyone got some pliers? I've been stuck here for *hours*.

. . . .

I was disappointed when I heard that William and Kate chose to name their first-born son – and the future king – 'George'. I was really hoping they would go with 'Joffrey'.

---

* Jenny Eclair: gobby comedian, now novelist.

Re: *Game of Thrones*

❶ Hodor.

❷ You summed up my feelings perfectly.

❸ Hodor!* Hodor!

Now That's What I Call Movies

....

Re: *Breakfast at Tiffany's*

Great how middle-class Guardianistas can read/watch romanticised/rose-tinted books/films about prostitution and describe them as 'escapism'.

....

Re: James Bond

GoldenEye. A film so 1990s they could have swapped Brosnan with Quentin Wilson from *Top Gear* and no one would have noticed.

....

---

* Hodor: Hodor, hodor. Hodor?

Re: *Back to the Future*

To this day I instantly assume anyone driving a VW camper is a Libyan terrorist.

. . . .

Re: *Predator*

It's big, it's dumb, it's ludicrously homo-erotic, it's military fetishism and it's massively right wing in tone. Bloody brilliant, it is.

. . . .

Re: Should we have more *Star Wars* films?

Just think how many nurses we could employ with all that money? Or food banks we could build?

. . . .

Re: *Some Like It Hot*

Poor man's *Nuns on the Run*.

. . . .

Re: *Ghostbusters*

You forgot the most 1980s thing about the whole film: the world is saved by a small business.

. . . .

Re: Aronofsky's *Noah*

It's obviously another pro-eugenics film coming out of the Hollywood fascist propaganda machine.

....

Re: *Muppets Most Wanted*

Gulags, mass murder and the concentration camp system: why are we allowed to laugh at this? [It shows] lack of taste and sensitivity for the suffering of millions of victims of Soviet terror. Next sequel: Muppets go to Mauthausen?

....

Re: New Flintstones Movies

Yabba dabba don't.

....

Re: *Spider-Man*

❶ So how does Spider-Man become Spider-Man then? Something to do with a spider I bet?

❷ He was a spider bitten by a radioactive man.

....

Re: *Star Wars*

Strange how most people get caught in the superstructure and do not understand or appreciate the layered, esoteric content and instruction that is the real substructure of the whole series. It is not the superficial action (of variable quality) that has captivated the public for almost 40 years but the archetypes within it that are also buried in the human psyche.

....

Re: *My Best Friend's Wedding*

Two hot women, one a sweet blonde, the other a 'difficult' brunette fighting for the love of a dull man. No thanks. If I want outdated sexist stereotypes, I don't have to pay to see them.

....

Re: *The Bodyguard*

Good god, no. I'd take a bullet instead of watching this!

....

Re: *The Bodyguard*

I misread the description of this film as containing a 'horrifying song', which is absolutely accurate.

....

Nosferatu probably seems a bit lame now that Iain
Duncan Smith is featuring so prominently in daily life.
We've been desensitised.

. . . .

Harry Potter's subtext is the subjugation of women
by an all-powerful, hidden patriarchy. The heroine of
the story is Hermione – who must adopt male traits in
order to battle the patriarchy for acceptance – despite
the added disadvantage of being of mixed birth. Harry
Potter is merely the foil for this great feminist work.

. . . .

Re: *Titanic* in 3D

Apparently you *can* polish a turd.

. . . .

❶ Michael Bay and Zack Snyder are among the most
under-appreciated directors working in Hollywood.

❷ What you say is 100% true, within the stripper and
adult entertainment community.

. . . .

Twins is a work of unfairly maligned genius.

I hated him before it was popular to do so.

. . . .

Forrest Gump has a running time of 142 minutes.
Cut out 141.5 minutes and leave the few bars of Jimi
Hendrix in the middle. That will improve it enormously.

. . . .

Re: *Django Unchained*

Am I the only one who thought it was a trite revenge
fantasy? Or the only one who had a problem with the
idea that the big bad guy in a movie about slavery was
a black slave? Or that the cartoonish nonsense so
admired by the reviewer here sat very uneasily with the
gruesome and serious depictions of slavery?

Now That's What I Call Proper Culture

. . . .

Re: What makes a good theatre date?

A nice snooze. I can't resist a good nap during a visit to
the theatre. Comfy seats, warmth, people talking in the
background – lovely.

. . . .

❶ It's very useful to have all these flag-waving, tub-thumping jingoists in one place at one time.

❷ Why does Nigel Kennedy have to turn up looking like Worzel Gummidge?

. . . .

Never pee in the basement at the Old Vic. They're AWFUL toilets. Even if I'm sitting in the stalls, I'll always go to the top level and use the ladies there.

. . . .

I once got free cheese at the bar in the Southwark Playhouse, which was outstanding.

. . . .

No one of any age should be made to watch *The Taming of the Shrew*. I think I'd need Ritalin to sit through it myself.

. . . .

❶ Just watching a series of Chaplin's Mutual Comedies on the Franco-German channel, Arte.

❷ Well, who isn't?

❸ I'm currently watching Jacques Tati on Serbo-Croat channel, Arse.

. . . .

❶ I would love to see more experimental/new theatre in local theatres.

❷ Well, I am frustrated by the increased number of experimental and modernist productions that are now put on at local places such as the Birmingham Rep and Warwick Arts Centre. I am an old-fashioned woman who wants to see classic 19th- and 20th-century plays.

. . . .

Re: Solving the problems of the West End

Want to solve the problem of a 'musical'? Cut the music. I believe it's then called a 'play', and it's quite a bit better.

Now That's What I Call Christmas TV

....

Judging by the casting line-up, it's another white Christmas on the BBC.

....

Just seen this year's schedule. No opera, no ballet, no classical music? Awful.

....

Re: Why would you read previews of Christmas TV?

It's always good having advance warning of a Lenny Henry appearance. It's really not nice when he takes you by surprise.

....

Having a show called *Pointless Celebrities* kind of sums things up really.

....

Can someone wake me up when *Das Boot** is on?

....

---

* *Das Boot*: German war film, possibly about shoes.

Orwell was right about the future. Imagine a boot stamping on a human face . . . or just watch *EastEnders* on Christmas Day.

....

Five Key Moments in this year's Christmas TV: 1. Turning telly-box on; 2. Flicking through the channels; 3. Deciding it's all repeats; 4. Turning telly-box off; 5. Reaching for a bottle of Bombay Sapphire and a volume of Proust.

....

Muppets Christmas Carol has to be watched on Christmas Eve or it will bring about the apocalypse. It's a moral duty.

Now That's What I Call *The Archers*
....

The Archers: the soap opera for posh people who can't stand the embarrassment of watching *Coronation Street*.

....

Re: What do the characters in *The Archers* listen to at 7 p.m. on Radio 4?

❶ Maybe they listen to *The Archers* too, but because it's the radio we don't realise which parts is just us listening to the radio on the radio, or us just listening to the radio. There might be one whole storyline that we think is part of the programme, but is actually a dialogue-free part of *The Archers* where we're just listening to their radios playing in the background.

❷ It's like a middle-class remake of *Inception*.

. . . .

Archers fans love a moan. We complain that there isn't enough farming info in it, then complain they keep banging on about outdoor milking vs robotic milking parlours. We moan nothing happens, then moan too much is happening. We beg them to stop going on about Tom's ready meals then have a fit when he buggers off and the ready meals are abandoned.

. . . .

I'm hoping that Lynda Snell will convert to Islam, cancel the panto, turn the village hall into a madrassa and impose sharia law on Bert, Kathy and Pip for their truly dreadful acting abilities. Just to shake up Middle England.

. . . .

Forget tuition fees, if you want to see riots and civil unrest in England tinker with the Sunday *Archers* omnibus on Radio 4.

. . . .

I love *The Archers* but whenever I have to explain why I have absolutely no idea.

. . . .

Re: Unresolved plots

I was concerned about Jill's bees, which she apparently abandoned. Perhaps that was part of another interminable plot, where, for lack of management, they swarm and kill someone.

. . . .

The 'Will and Ed' feud is one of *The Archers*' dullest storylines. Which is quite an achievement considering the competition.

. . . .

It's just *Jeremy Kyle* in second-hand Barbour jackets and a whiff of Swarfega*

---

* Swarfega: super-powered soap used by farmers, mechanics, plumbers and truckers. It smells like hard work.

The *Archers*' editor has much in common with David Cameron. Both are custodians of an institution dear to the hearts of Middle England, are bereft of new ideas and are now, like some desperate old band, rehashing their greatest hits from the 80's. All we can do is suffer.

. . . .

The Archers is a big advert for the doomed meat and dairy industries. We need a few vegan Greens as serious characters to balance this skewed and misguided view of the highly subsidised and destructive farming practices in GB plc.

. . . .

Was far, far better when it was all 'Ooh arrr, Master Phil', casseroles and heavy-handed Min. of Ag. warble-fly reminders.*

---

* All right, sorry, I have literally no idea what any of this means, but it got a lot of 'Recommends' on the website. It's probably got something to do with Nigel falling off the roof that time (almost every other comment is about that, so it's a good guess).

9
Spot the Ball

....

Certain subjects can be considered toxic to internet conversations, as anyone who has ever read our 'Poem of the Week' column will know. However nothing, nothing, starts arguments like sport. By its very nature it is the most partisan, shouty, gloriously combustible section of the entire site and when a big event happens, such as a certain Uruguayan footballer getting a bit bitey, or a certain Scottish/British [delete as applicable] grumpy tennis player crashing out of a major tournament, the internet fair explodes. Happily the sport community is also filled with less volatile little corners, full of people talking lovingly about cricket, racing, cycling or curling with an endearing passion for the most niche of sports. Anyone for fencing, or lacrosse?

The Beautiful Game

....

I can't be the only one who hates the football for delaying *Toy Story 3* by a bloody month [for the World Cup]. Isn't this enough to prove our country has priorities mixed?

....

Re: Ian Botham's football career

I saw Botham play at Hull's old ground in the 1980s. To say he was a footballer was stretching it a bit. He had the stomach of Micky Quinn, the stamina of Özil and the touch of Carlton Palmer.

....

If a player has been at a club for a minimum of 10 years, then badge kissing can be allowed. If they haven't and they do it, yellow card.

....

Why does the orchestra play 'The Great Escape'
despite England being three–nil up? What should we
be escaping from? Who are you trying to encourage?

....

I hate the shoddy way the FA Cup Final is now treated.
What happened to the build? Starting with what the
players had for breakfast, interviews with the assistant
physio, team buses leaving the hotel, etc?

....

I didn't believe it was possible that our contribution to
the World Cup could be worse than our contribution
to the Eurovision Song Contest, but it is by some
distance. That takes some doing.

....

When a country wins the World Cup trophy three times
they get to keep the trophy permanently. If Brazil wins
the new trophy three times then they will have collected
three World Cup trophies and will be declared the
ultimate winners of the football. It will finally have been
decided who has won the football, and football will end.

....

❶ We French love to rubbish the English about their national football team, their train system and, more than anything else, their hypocrisy.

❷ But we English hate the England football team more than you could ever dream of doing.

. . . .

If Manchester United had passed the ball accurately as often as this writer includes subordinate phrases in her sentences, David Moyes might still be manager.

Four Wheels Good, Two Wheels Better

. . . .

Re: Lance Armstrong

I think Lance should be applauded for winning the Tour de France. When I took shed loads of drugs I couldn't even *find* my bicycle.

. . . .

Re: Bradley Wiggins

This man was knighted for riding a bike? The mind boggles.

. . . .

❶ They think they are touring France when really they are in Yorkshire. What drugs are they on?

❷ Dangerous question to ask when discussing professional cycling . . .

. . . .

Re: The Tour de France Yorkshire leg

❶ A word of warning to anyone going to watch. I wasn't paying attention as the caravan passed by and got hit in the eye by a flying baguette.

❷ Such a complete authentic French experience it could almost be marketed as a *Guardian* holiday.

. . . .

Re: Dangerous cyclists on the road

I'm yet to meet a single 'boy racer' who also has a bell.

Leather on Willow

. . . .

Re: Baseball v cricket

If the game's not on Radio 4 Long Wave, I'm against it.

Being one of England's most successful one-day players? That's a bit like being one of Germany's funniest comedians.

. . . .

England have learned to snatch defeat from the jaws of victory in every format of the game. It is really quite an achievement.

. . . .

My last girlfriend did ask me once if I would rather play cricket than have sex (expecting me to say 'have sex'). I think I hesitated too long when giving the answer; she wasn't happy.

. . . .

Re: Cricket v football

❶ I'd like to see Robbie Savage facing Mitchell Johnson.

❷ Or a firing squad . . .

. . . .

Re: Test cricket v Twenty20

If Test cricket is the opera, full of subtle movements and changes of momentum, of unbridled passion and utter despair, then IPL is punk rock, a sudden sharp burst of noise, sound and fury with the occasional hint of skill.

. . . .

Is cricket the only field in which Australians are always appealing?

. . . .

Re: Test cricket played at night

❶ I'm wondering what they will call the 'intervals'. I'm assuming that after the first session everyone still comes off for tea, but for how long? Will the second meal break be 'supper', or 'midnight munchies' perhaps? A bowl of soup and a spot of cheese on toast? These things are important and need clarifying!

❷ Could be entertaining listening to the commentary – can't imagine Ian Botham being able to stay sober until the end of play.

. . . .

I had a superstition about fielding at short leg after tea when egg sandwiches were served.

Fighting Talk

....

Pah, cage fighting? Easy peasy. All you need is a sturdy pair of bolt cutters. They don't even try and run away.

....

I see the popularity of 'cage fighting' as being part of the decline of Western civilisation. Just like Rome watching gladiator fights as its society crumbled, mixed martial arts is a sign of decadence and decline.

....

The human race is in crisis, if you think men twatting each other is sport and entertainment. Nobody deserves respect, only pity.

....

If Djokovic, Nadal, Murray and Federer all took to prancing about with huge belts on, all claiming they were world champions while doing everything they could to avoid playing each other, I would think tennis was a complete and utter joke.

. . . .

I liked that wrestling you used to see on *World of Sport* where big, bearded, middle-aged fat men in one-piece bathing-suits jumped on each other and the grannies in the audience tried to join in.

The Olympics, Summer
. . . .

Can people stop using 'medal' as a verb?

. . . .

Coldplay [at the Closing Ceremony] have just ruined the whole Olympics.

. . . .

Re: What is the legacy of the 2012 Games for you?

A mild sense of ennui.

Amid the artificially induced euphoria, I'd like to remind people to keep an eye out for bad news that will be buried in the coming weeks.

. . . .

Re: Dressage

Evidently the horses also get a plaque that they can attach to their stable . . . not sure how they do this with their hoofs (hooves?).

. . . .

Oh Jesus Christ! There are *morris dancers* out there! Take that, Beijing!

. . . .

If the rich, private-school, Oxbridge types pole-danced it would have been in the Olympics years ago.

The Olympics, Winter

. . . .

Lots of different ways of sliding around.

. . . .

You do wonder what on earth we're trying to prove by putting public money into winning medals at tobogganing?

New Balls Please

. . . .

Andy Murray – the first British man to win the Wimbledon men's singles championship wearing shorts.

Outrageous: I believe Federer was told off for having orange soles on his tennis shoes, but not a word to Sharapova over her orange knickers. Give me strength.

. . . .

I just don't have the patience to sit there watching somebody repeatedly failing to do something which they could do every time if they had to.

. . . .

What's happened to the single-handed backhand? Cliff Drysdale has a lot to answer for.

. . . .

She is the Phil 'The Power' Taylor of female tennis.

. . . .

Surely it's not beyond the wit of man to come up with hard courts that are a bit . . . y'know, softer on the knees?

Funny-shaped Balls, Please

....

Rugby is so tedious the fans applaud when the ball is booted off the pitch.

....

Look at the shape of the ball – no wonder they have to carry it.

....

I used to enjoy watching rugby, but I suffer from paranoia and every time they huddled down for a scrum I thought they were talking about me. It all became too much.

....

I love the *haka* but feel the English should be able to respond in kind, with their own traditional battle chants.

....

If you can't enjoy the upcoming Wales v England game, you must be dead: war without bullets, beauty and the beast. I cannot wait.

....

Everyone in New Zealand *has* to agree to 'Like' the All Blacks or they're not allowed a Facebook account.

Smackdown!

....

Wrestling is to art what Snickers bars are to food.

. . . .

Re: Wrestler Darren Young coming out as gay

❶ Do WWE wrestlers not have stage names any more?

❷ Yeah, they do! His real name is Lightning Geriatric.

. . . .

❶ Since when were actors in a scripted show athletes?

❷ Since Stone Cold said so.

. . . .

Lardy blokes flopping around on the floor to a pre-planned script? It's called Westminster.

10
Why on Earth
Would Anyone . . .

··

There's one question that unites internet commenters everywhere, and especially on the *Guardian*. It's the ultimate question, not the one about Life, the Universe and Everything, but even more profound, even more important than that. Five little words that express more bewilderment, disdain, curiosity or joyous disbelief than any other in the English language . . . That question is: 'Why on earth would anyone . . .'

Why on earth would anyone, given the choice, watch ITV?

. . . .

Why on earth would anyone iron their underwear?

. . . .

Why on earth would anyone want to do DIY when there
are so many unemployed plumbers and carpenters?

. . . .

Why on earth do people still 'live' in Gateshead?

. . . .

Why on earth would anyone have five Ramones
albums? Once you've bought the first one, you've got
them all.

. . . .

Why on earth would anyone believe what is written in
the Liberal Democrat manifesto?

❶ Why on earth would anyone want to have sex on a rose-petalled bed?

❷ As my partner suffers from acute and quite spectacular hay fever, I must confess that I have zero direct experience either of petal-strewn beds or rolls in the hay.

❸ Well, certainly not me. I do all the housework and would have to hoover the bloody things up after.

....

Why on earth would anyone put chicken on a pizza? Seriously, that sounds disgusting. Tomato, mozzarella and basil – yes. Chicken – no.

....

Why on earth would anyone only use skimmed milk?

....

Re: Tea served in coffee shops

Why on earth would anyone go to Starbucks for the imperial beverage?

....

Why on earth would anyone want to learn how to make a Victoria sponge? They're pale, dry, tasteless and, to quote my grandmother, 'only fit for public exhibition'.

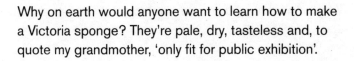

Why on earth would anyone try to produce a *fluffy* chip? They are supposed to be heavy. They sit comfortably overnight on the five pints consumed earlier, thus preventing dizziness and nausea, enabling one to awake fresh and alert in the morning.

❶ Why on earth would anyone want to drink booze at work?

❷ Same reason for masturbating at work: it's fun, and you get paid for it.

❸ Can I get a job in the place where you work? Oh, on second thoughts . . .

❷ I actually work as a life model for art classes, so masturbating at work is somewhat difficult.

Why on earth would anyone want the head of what was once a living being on their wall? Would they also hang a human head?

Why on earth would anyone want to meet George Galloway,* and then spend time talking to him?

· ·

Re: MPs' expenses

❶ Why on earth would anyone need three garlic crushers? How can that be a justified MP's expense?

❷ One for his constituency home, one for his London home, and one for whipping up a spot of aioli during a commute?

---

* George Galloway: politician and reality TV cat impersonator.

Why on earth would anyone want to put his penis into a toaster?

. . . .

Why on earth would anyone need an app for masturbation? People were happily doing it long before there were mobile phones. Really, that's the great thing about masturbating – anyone can do it.

. . . .

Why on earth would anyone use Microsoft Internet Explorer if they had a choice?

. . . .

Why on earth would anyone even want to meet footballers? Most of them haven't got two GCSEs to rub together.

. . . .

Why on earth would anyone derive pleasure from golf caddying?

. . . .

Why on earth would anyone take advice from someone called 'Venice A. Fulton'? It sounds like a range of bidets.

. . . .

Why on earth would anyone try to estimate the number of Aussies with an Irish granny?

. . . .

Re: Strepsils' Facebook page

Why on earth would anyone want to be faux friends with a cough lozenge?

. . . .

Why on earth would anyone want to go to Vegas with Olly Murs? Unless they were planning on re-enacting an episode of *CSI* where a really annoying hat-wearing pop star dies in mysterious circumstances . . .

. . . .

Why on earth would anyone want to see Ricky Gervais in HD?

. . . .

Why on earth would anyone want to buy a mug of an old man's mug?

. . . .

Why on earth would anyone want to work in 'middle management of a large company'? Have you met these people?

. . . .

Why on earth would anyone want the Blairs anywhere near them on their wedding day?

. . . .

Why on earth would anyone buy a wooden bike? Very uncomfortable and splinters in your arse. No, thanks!

. . . .

Why on earth would anyone beat up a tree?

. . . .

Why on earth would anyone want to watch TV on the loo?

. . . .

Why on earth would anyone want to drink lager in the UK? It resembles gnat's piss – both in colour and taste – that has to be chilled to near freezing just to make it close to palatable. British real ale, well kept by a real publican, lightly effervescent and at cellar temperature so the full aroma and flavour can come out, is the greatest beer in the world.

. . . .

Why on earth would anyone be jealous of a golfer?

. . . .

Why on earth would anyone type 'big Asian ass' into a search? The donkey is indigenous to Africa. *E. Africanus Asinus*.

. . . .

Re: New high-speed rail link between London and Birmingham

But why on earth would anyone want to go to Birmingham?

. . . .

❶ Why on earth would anyone see being short as some sort of defect that has to be corrected by high heels?

❷ Because I haven't perfected the art of levitation yet.

. . . .

Why on earth would anyone be watching football when there's a cracking *Midsomer Murders* repeat on ITV1?

. . . .

Why on earth would anyone want to encourage the youth to vote?

. . . .

Why on earth would anyone want to live in Monte Carlo when they could be living in Swansea or Hull?

. . . .

Why on earth would anyone buy salad dressing when it's so easy to make?

. . . .

Why on earth would anyone need a recipe for crisp sandwiches?

. . . .

Why on earth would anyone want to socialise with the people they work with?

. . . .

Why on earth would anyone absolutely ruin Turkish delight by covering it in chocolate?

. . . .

Why on earth would anyone want a Big Mac before midday?

. . . .

Why on earth would anyone queue for Starbucks?

. . . .

Why on earth would anyone marry a philosopher?

Acknowledgements

....

We'd like to thank the brilliant *Guardian* commenters (listed below) whose contributions are included in this book. Their wit, energy and world view made this project and indeed our whole website, a delight to read and work on:

1nn1t, aalmenara, Abdullah Abdi, aboleth, ABZ321, agedlady, AgentKitson, alanredangel, alb1on, Albert Ravey, albion08, Alex239, alexanderolive, alexandraUB, alexito, Alfresco11, Alfster, aliendrum, alimantado, alldoomed, alloomis, ally07, AllyF, Ameliascottage, amsams, Andrew Lawton, andyrev, AnnElke, aoife101, AppleFan, Approveds, Apresmoiledeluge, areader10, AreYouOnMute, ariel3, Arnemetius, arosoff, arpies, ArseneKnows, ArthurTheCat, astgameplayer, attila9000, Avongirl, AwesomeCroc, AzuraTheBlueDevil, BabyJonker, BaggiosChip, Baldbob Belling, Banditolobster, BarbarianAtTheGate, BarneyQ, Baron Barrington Effenbad III, BaronGrovelville, Barrier, Barry Minge, BarryHercules1979, BarryJames, bartletsjacket, beaupuss, beccajane, beccalikesbooks, BeckyDavidson, beeanchor, beegdawg007, beltfedwombat, BenCaute, Benulek, BigBear63, BigDukeSix, bigworv, billysbar, bishbosh, BlamedForWhat, blighty, bllckchps, blueguitarman, Blusoulman, bobbysixty, Bob Helpful, bobinchiclana, Bobshaw2, bobsyouruncle1, BombNumber20, borisoftickfen, borleg, BornInBrighton1968, boynamedstu, BOURAGH, bradgate, Brandybuck, breisleach, BrianIreland, brimble, BristolBoy, Broomersp, Bullgod, BurgermaS, CageRider, camdencarrot, captainunsensible, CaptCrash, caracol, caskconditioned, Catch22, caterinadisiena, causeoreffect, CelticSaint, CentralBelter, cerealcat, cerises, champ16ns, Chazza, cheddarfiend, Chloe1066, chm4lm, Chris Icarus, Chris Swan, ChrisBenton, chrisjhutch11, christabelaroo, clarissadesward, ClarkEKhat, clivejw, cockermouth, Collywobbles, combot35, CompassionateTory, Composer, ConfuciusHeSay, conifer2, Conor Maverick Mallen, Consortium11, CordwainerBird, Cosmodemon, CouchSlob, CountlessElizabeth, craigtherage, crouchyvixxxen69, CrypticMirror, cymbula, DafyddApHugh, DameHedwig, Dan Gatliff, DanielBurden, danjc93, DanSmith, daveweston, daveydor, davidabsalom, David Adlington, David Bana, David Bromley, davidiain, davidjjknowles, dcwishart, DeConstruct, DeepSlumber, defragmentation, defusenik, deiseach, depad65, Desmond Miles, dfishman, Diana Price, dieter2602, dipole, dirtybadger, DistortedViola, DolleDolf, DollyRotten, doriela, DorkingBoy, Dormsville, DrabWilly, DrJazz, DrTriflephd, Dryhtscipe, dudemanguy, DunkirkPi, dunmail, Dweezle, Dylanwolf, EastFinchleyite, eerwego, eggiebread, eggstatic, el0villano, elbowgrease, elephantwoman, elmondo2012, elmsyrup, EmersonsIPA, emmcol, Endeavour7, EricPickLess, Esco91, evangelink, Fakecharitybuster, falzmania, farabundovive, farfrom, FarsleyBantam, FastGamePlayer, FatherNoelFurlong, FearTheKittens, feeling, femalelefty, Fergus Brown, Fezz76, figbat, FJ1000, foolwhoknows, Forestlands, frankiecrisp, FrDuffyFighting69th, freepoland, fridgeman, frindsbury, fripouille, frosty3010, Fuchsiagrower, furbossina, futdashukup, fuzzgin, Galaxina, Gallinaingles, gaswoman, Gav67, gb76uk, GCday, Geht Euch Nicht An, geoeeee, GeoffTr, GeorgeOilwell84, George White, gerard1marks, gfpdiehn, gibtardo, Giftedcynic, GilbertTheAlien, gironomo55, giveusaclue, Glammerocity, glendoan, Glen Pierce, GMonet, Gooner67, Gordonbnt, GordonBrown12, GordonLiddle, grafittilessons, Grampie, greensox, Grimo1, gruniadreader666, gullibletraveller, haardvark, halfeatern, HandandShrimp, HappyPal, HappyValley, harangutan2006, hardatwork, HarryTheHorse, HeathCardwell, HeatherR, Heavycola, heedtracker, Hegelian, hellopaul, HelloPoorPeople, hermionegingold, hexgar, hiccup1, Hol48, holdingahighline, holzy, Hooloovoo, Hundred and Ten Percent, hydroxyl, iainl, iamtherobotman, IceCreamTony, ID0820762, ID3271332, ID4719109, ID6219391, ID7776906, IgnatiusJacques, IgorBeaver, imalwaysangry2, imdjam, Imorse, IndependentLady, inmufti, inrange, Isaachunt60, ItsAnOutrage2, itshokukonane, IvanTiger, IzzyMoreno,

jackheron, Jacqueline Gemini Honeybee, jae426,
Jairzhino, James Ley, JamesMM, jameswilson4000, Jane
Duncan Thurlow, JasonStephenBarlow, jayemp,
JBGrenouille, JBPriestly, jbrag, Jen Robinson,
JennieKermode, JestersDead, JezKeen, JGradyCole,
Jimbojimbo, JimdeB, jlr26170, Joe Turner, joelgion, John
Tarr, johncrowe, Johnl, JohnnyNunsuchArisen,
JohnTMaher, JohnTy66, JohnYardDog, JolyonWagg,
Jonna Sercombe, Jonty Wilks, jptoc, jstone, JTzara,
Jumpinoverhoops, justablokw, kaff, Keith Cunningham,
kellyseyenumberone, Kemster, kendrew, khongor,
KingCrud, Kippps, kisunssi, kloxile, Knitterbird, Kovich,
kristinekochanski, KrawuziKapuzi, kursteinwanker, Kyle
Whittall, LabanTall, LadyC, ladymarmalade, Lakshmanab,
lambofgod, lansing, LaxativeFunction, legalman,
lexcredendi, Lexicon1, Leonnoel, Leopold1904,
Lhur2006, liamkl, limu, LionelMessias, lissendis,
LiviaDrusilla, llamalpaca, lloydslondon,
logisticalnightmare, longpete, LordMeowingtons,
losttheremote, LouisaLou, LoveActuary, lowlyseer,
lporter, LTOtt, lucitex, lusucanna, Lycidas,
LyzlowGrzybowski, M Wilson, macisadog, madbobwillis,
Madranon, Maentwrog, maidenover, makinavajar,
mamahuhu, maninthemoon, ManofConstantSorrow,
MarieCurie, Mark Mclauchlan, markwallace,
MarmaladeQueen, Marsman72, Martin_C, MartinRDB,
martinusher, MartyMcFlytipper, matt70380,
mattmcneany, Maugrim, mawhite, maxfisher,
MaxTurbotron, MCA van Loenen, mccartney77,

MelanieDubliner, Meranerin, mergatroidohara, Meristem, Merperson, metalvendetta, MichaelBulley, michaelmichael, MickGJ, Micktrick, mignonette, Mike Brown, mikedow, MikeRichards, mikio44, MisterRed, MisterSquiddy, Monchberter, moneyallgone, MoreTears, moretheylie, Morey91, Mornex74, Morninglight, Morph81, Moryu, MostUncivilised, mototom, moules, MountEtna, MoveAnyMountain, MrSHolmes, MsHedgehog, MsJess, MsRobinson, murdamcloud, Murmur, muscleguy, Musetta, mushyp, Mutterer, mysensephalon, MysteryTor, MZorin, nacom, nails7, Nanea, Narin Bahar, nega9000, neilmac1921, NeitherYankNorBri, NeXTNY, Niall0007, Nic Price, nigelbryan, NoahDeere, nocausetoaddopt, nocod, NorfolkBoy, Norris667, Northumbriana, Nosnhoj, NotWithoutMyMonkey, nzgirluk, Odicean, offshoretomorrow, oggaman, ohagandaaz, ohandanotherthing, one gonk, operationjulie, Oranje14, originaltitle, OttoMaddox, Owlyross, PacoFleyas, PadraigOHooligan, pandachops, ParcelOfRogue, PariahCarefree, PatriciaPJ, paulhs, pbendall, peopleisstupid, peppermintish, Peridot, PeteBr, Phillyguy, Phud, pickledhennings, PierreGn, pikeman, PinkChocolate, pithyblogname, Plummy, plurien, PoliceDefective, Polymorph, pommyb, poppy23, P_R_Proudhon, prankmonkey, pretendname, PriscillaX, ProfessorPlums, Pubbore, Publunch, puntoebasta, Purity, Puss, Quackersyard, quittoexit, R042, Rachelthedigger, Racje, radical, Ragnor, Raya Speed, rdrr, Reynard the Fox, rhinestonecowgirl, rickylee369, RoaroftheSevernBore, Robert Vorthman, Robstacle, RollandLeRat, Roosterbooster198, RossCovert, rottiesteve, Rotwatcher, rowett, rukiddingme2, ruskiny, RustyHarpoon, Sachertorte, sailthedarkenedseas, saintpellegrino, saintzeno, Sallyroberts, SamGamgee, sammsmith, Samvara, Sandmaennchen, Scamander2, Sceptic101, SchmuckOnWheels, Seastaugh, selosra, SergeantBash, Setanta4Now, sfk2, shauny, showmaster, sillyknut, silverkaite, Simgeo, SimonG1, SimonGhent, simonmaxwell, SimonMobileDisco, sirchutneyroars, SirWiggo, skipissatan, skyearthwinda, SleepieHead, sloftslime, snakeoilsalesman, Snarlygog, snowybutfine, sociablesocialist, socialistnotnulabour, SonOfTheDesert, sosprey, southcombe, Spacedone, Spikediswhack, SPLD, splendido, Spoonface, Stabbo2, Starfcker, startingover, Steff Clarke, stepney52, Steve Bagley, StevieWeegie, stoneface1, StrawBear, StrokerAce, Strollinby, Strummered, StuartRG, stupidwise, subprime, sunds, SuperAiChan, SuperGarryMonk, SValmont, swedishyorkie, Synchronisity, TabloidScum, Tamar123, tarahill3, taraibiza, Tarantella, teaandchocolate, Tehillim, tektok, TenWhoWereTaken, Terence Cass, texavery, tezzad, Thanosi, thatwoggirlcallie, The_Truth_Hurts, TheDogShouterer, THE GRANDINQUISIT0R, TheIndian777, TheJoyOfEssex, TheStowE17, TheTruthisaLie, TheVeggieBurgher, theWeeb, ThisIsMyEighthName, ThisLeeNoble, ThomasBetham, thornbush, ThreeCookies, throwawayaccount2, tigerm,

TissueOfFlies, TobyLatimer, TodayIamtheZodiac, tomsito, tooskintogotocuba, trentp, trinder19, tristanmax, TruculentSheep, TVwriter, tweetiepie16, unaszplodrmann, unclearleo, Unconstituted, unhombredesw19, unleaded, Unobtanium, upgrayedd85, urardo, Urmston86, valdez, vomittingmeerkat, vonZeppelin, voodoo22, VSLVSL, waitingtopounce, wasson, Waterkanter, Wellesz, Whataniceman, whatithink, whood, wightangler, Willbox, willmau5, windbag, Wiretrip, Wolf44Blues, wooablackbetty, wordtaster, YeOldeSoothsayer, YevgenyChar, YorkerBouncer, yoyobear, yoyoga, Zakelius, Zakida, zeefor, Zuvtawov943

Huge thanks as ever to the *Guardian* Communities team, past and present, especially Ed Hadfield, Joanna Geary, Mary Hamilton and the ever supportive Laura Oliver. Special thanks must go to my colleagues on the long-suffering and thoroughly under-appreciated Moderation team.

Thanks too for the co-operation and support of Sheila Pulham, Jan Thompson, Kath Viner and Alan Rusbridger.

Much appreciation is due to Laura Hassan at Guardian Faber whose patience and support in this project and its editor has pulled it through from inception.

Finally, thanks and love to Emma Dalby Bowler who, a decade on, is still keeping me from going quite, quite mad.